Management, Organization, and Childbirth

Management, Organization, and Childbirth: Towards a New Model for the Birth Path explores the complex topic of the birth path with a multidisciplinary magnifying glass on the paradigms, languages, and tools critical to the organization, management, and clinical science.

The work consists of five chapters. The first chapter provides a multidimensional analysis of childbirth. The second chapter presents an organizational analysis that moves in unison with different models of health. The third chapter studies the birth path in organizational and clinical terms by describing it in its core processes. The fourth chapter proposes a study conducted in the Italian context, which identifies some useful determinants for redesigning the birth path. The fifth chapter formulates a proposal for redesigning the birth path based on a new health paradigm.

The proposed model offers useful insights for multiple categories of readers. To students of medicine and higher education tracks in healthcare management, it can offer opportunities to raise awareness not only regarding multiprofessional practice but also regarding confrontation with complementary disciplines. To practitioners and policy makers, it can provide useful stimuli to promote rational and informed decisions around the childbirth. To researchers studying the health context within different disciplinary domains, the model can offer unexplored research spaces within the new business complex system.

Gabriella Piscopo PhD in Public Management, is Associate Professor of Organization Studies, Scientific Director of the "Observatory on Organizational Behavior and Life Skills", Deputy Director of the "Leadership and Digital Transformation" Master at the University of Salerno, Italy. She is Management Trainer and Scientific Coordinator of several research projects on Healthcare, Judicial System and Complex Organizations.

Margherita Ruberto is PhD in Big Data Management at the University of Salerno, Italy. She is an expert collaborator at AGENAS – National Agency for Regional Health Services (PON Governance e Capacità Istituzionale 2014-2020)

Routledge studies in health management
Edited by Ewan Ferlie

The healthcare sector is now of major significance, economically, scientifically and societally. In many countries, healthcare organizations are experiencing major pressures to change and restructure, while cost containment efforts have been accentuated by global economic crisis. Users are demanding higher service quality, and healthcare professions are experiencing significant reorganization whilst operating under increased demands from an ageing population.

Critically analytic, politically informed, discursive and theoretically grounded, rather than narrowly technical or positivistic, the series seeks to analyze current healthcare organizations. Reflecting the intense focus of policy and academic interest, it moves beyond the day to day debate to consider the broader implications of international organizational and management research and different theoretical framings.

Making Sense of Organizational Change and Innovation in Health Care
An Everyday Ethnography
Anne Reff Pedersen

Innovating Healthcare
The Role of Political, Managerial and Clinical Leadership
John Storey and Richard Holti

Co-production and Japanese Healthcare
Work Environment, Governance, Service Quality and Social Values
Victor A. Pestoff

Management, Organization, and Childbirth
Towards a New Model for the Birth Path
Gabriella Piscopo and Margherita Ruberto

Management, Organization, and Childbirth

Towards a New Model for the Birth Path

Gabriella Piscopo and Margherita Ruberto

NEW YORK AND LONDON

First published 2023
by Routledge
605 Third Avenue, New York, NY 10158

and by Routledge
4 Park Square, Milton Park, Abingdon, Oxon, OX14 4RN

Routledge is an imprint of the Taylor & Francis Group, an informa business

© 2023 Gabriella Piscopo and Margherita Ruberto

The right of Gabriella Piscopo and Margherita Ruberto to be identified as author[/s] of this work has been asserted in accordance with sections 77 and 78 of the Copyright, Designs and Patents Act 1988.

All rights reserved. No part of this book may be reprinted or reproduced or utilised in any form or by any electronic, mechanical, or other means, now known or hereafter invented, including photocopying and recording, or in any information storage or retrieval system, without permission in writing from the publishers.

Trademark notice: Product or corporate names may be trademarks or registered trademarks, and are used only for identification and explanation without intent to infringe.

ISBN: 978-1-032-36065-2 (hbk)
ISBN: 978-1-032-36066-9 (pbk)
ISBN: 978-1-003-33009-7 (ebk)

DOI: 10.4324/9781003330097

Typeset in Bembo
by MPS Limited, Dehradun

Contents

List of figures viii
List of tables ix
Foreword x
Acknowledgments xiii

Introduction 1

1 The multidisciplinary nature of childbirth 4
GABRIELLA PISCOPO AND MARGHERITA RUBERTO

   1.1 *Defining aspects and characteristics of the birth path 4*
   1.2 *Social context: the social determinants and epidemiology of birth path 5*
   1.3 *Technological context: the tools to support the birth path 7*
   1.4 *The multidisciplinary debate in the international scenario 10*
   References 11

2 The managerial and organizational perspective of healthcare 18
GABRIELLA PISCOPO

   2.1 *Management profiles in healthcare: health paradigms and institutional approaches 18*
      2.1.1 *Complexity and variability of healthcare 18*
      2.1.2 *Healthcare reforms and myths 19*
   2.2 *The organizational perspective of healthcare 21*
   2.3 *Process management in healthcare 25*
   2.4 *The organizational approach of patient-centeredness 29*

2.5 Healthcare process redesign and the challenge for the birth path 32
References 34

3 The birth path as a process: criticalities and cesarean section   41
GABRIELLA PISCOPO AND MARGHERITA RUBERTO

3.1 The stages of the birth path 41
3.2 Preconception care 41
3.3 Access to the birth path 43
3.4 Low-risk pregnancy pathway and medium-/high-risk pregnancy pathway 44
3.5 Labor and delivery 47
3.6 Puerperium 49
3.7 Cesarean section and medicalization of pregnancy 51
    3.7.1 Known medical risk factors 54
    3.7.2 Social and demographic factors 54
    3.7.3 Professional practice styles factors 55
    3.7.4 Factors influencing maternal decision-making 55
    3.7.5 Organizational factors 56
    3.7.6 Economic factors 56
    3.7.7 Cultural factors 57
References 58

4 Italian experience in the international context: empirical evidence from two case studies   69
GABRIELLA PISCOPO AND MARGHERITA RUBERTO

4.1 Introduction to case studies 69
    4.1.1 The Italian context 70
    4.1.2 Theoretical foundation: the T.R.E.E. model 71
    4.1.3 Data collection 73
    4.1.4 Data analysis 75
4.2 Results 81
4.3 Discussion 82
References 84

5 Towards a new model for the birth path   87
GABRIELLA PISCOPO

5.1 Redesigning the birth path: toward a new model 87

5.2 *Distributed health literacy and empowerment in the birth path* 90
5.3 *ICT as a clinical and managerial support tool* 92
5.4 *Conclusions and implications for academic literature on healthcare organizations* 93
References 94

Index 100

Figures

2.1	The professional bureaucracy	23
2.2	The process approach within the healthcare context	28
3.1	The Value Systems in the birth path	42
3.2	Preconception phase	43
3.3	Access to the birth pathway phase	45
3.4	Low-risk pregnancy pathway and medium-/high-risk pregnancy pathway	46
3.5	Labor and delivery phase	48
3.6	Puerperium phase	50
5.1	A Value Constellation for the birth path	88

Tables

3.1	Robson's classification	53
4.1	Sample characteristics	73
4.2	Hospital 1's DRG, weight, threshold, and ordinary admissions	75
4.3	Hospital 2's DRG, weight, threshold, and ordinary admissions	75
4.4	Mode of delivery and mode of labor contingency table	76
4.5	Mode of delivery and mode of labor chi-square test	76
4.6	Mode of delivery and professional condition contingency table	77
4.7	Mode of delivery and professional condition chi-square test	77
4.8	Mode of delivery and maternal age contingency table	77
4.9	Mode of delivery and maternal age chi-square test	78
4.10	Mode of delivery and title of study contingency table	78
4.11	Mode of delivery and title of study chi-square test	78
4.12	Mode of delivery and previous conceptions contingency table	79
4.13	Mode of delivery and previous conceptions chi-square test	79
4.14	Group statistics: mode of delivery and number of cesarean sections	79
4.15	Independent-samples test	80

Foreword

The exogenous shock brought about by the COVID-19 pandemic unleashed, in the health sector, an energy at once both destructive and generative. On the one hand, it has left behind a dramatic toll in terms of human lives and unflattering results in terms of risk management. Despite the fact that risk now represents the global horizon within which both individuals and organizations move, the so-called risk society, as christened by Ulrich Beck, had to take some hard knocks, especially when SARS-CoV-2 overlapped with chronic diseases.

On the other hand, the pandemic shock has fostered the ability to look at phenomena with a multifocal lens capable of viewing the healthcare context from a big-picture perspective while grasping the value and contribution that each organizational and social cell can provide to the holistic dimension of care. Since the onset of the pandemic, the need to enrich the healthcare management debate with the vision provided by other disciplines, including those in the biological, biomedical, and biosocial fields, which, while providing arguments and scientific evidence over the years on the risks associated with the disruption of natural balances, have often gone unheeded.

A clear, albeit merciless, snapshot of the global post-pandemic scenario was offered at the 75th World Assembly of the WHO in May 2022. Director-General Tedros Adhanom Ghebreyesus, in commenting on the World Health Statistics 2022 data, emphasized the dual speed of health systems' evolution and related innovation while acknowledging the sharpening of health inequality between rich and poor. Still far off, and still well beyond the 2023 time horizon set by WHO, is the "triple billion" goal of extending universal health coverage to one billion more people, protecting one billion more people from health emergencies, and ensuring better health and well-being for one billion more people.

Nonetheless, within the ashes of the pandemic devastation that has equally engulfed the health, economic, and social sectors, it is possible to incubate some sprouts of human-serving innovation.

The current liquidity of the socio-health context makes it possible to promote new cultural paradigms, renewed models and systems of intra- and inter-organizational relations, and unprecedented spaces for dialog and co-design between different domains capable of stimulating clinical, organizational, and technological innovation.

A first sprout of innovation is to be found in the virtuous orchestration of value between different cultures and contexts: between medicine and management; between organization, biology, and bioethics; between hospital and territory; between public and private; and between institutions and life science industries. After all, it is precisely the result of this value orchestration that has generated an antidote which, even before any vaccine, enabled healthcare organizations to deal with the uncertainty of the epidemiological framework by activating the antibodies of agile and resilient innovation.

The text presented by the authors, Gabriella Piscopo and Margherita Ruberto, represents a challenging attempt to activate the space of multidomain co-design that, through the contribution of organizational, managerial, and clinical vision, feeds a new logos around the birth path.

An initial process of decompacting the disciplinary visions applied to the childbirth event, through first organizational diagnosis and then clinical analysis, leads to recomposing the individual phases by reconfiguring them in a new dimension. The vision of motherhood that guides the analysis is that of a life-changing event for the woman that also strongly impacts the entire social-welfare system. The microcosm of childbirth thus sees narrow boundaries expanded, carefully drawn around the woman, welcoming the family and social network in the role of co-producers. Childbirth is placed at the center of a complex business system that contemplates initiatives to support the woman, the couple, and the unborn child, while also extending its action to the evolution of the individual and his or her health.

The rampant flow of digital technologies even within the experience of pregnancy projects the birth journey into the dimension defined by Luciano Floridi as "on-life," where real life and digital life coexist. Rapidly flowing communication along the different stages of the birth path travels on multiple, multilevel ICT channels and structures. A new philosophy of information awaits, therefore, to take shape specifically within the childbirth dimension.

The proposed organizational reconfiguration model for the birth path can activate multidisciplinary innovation thrusts. However, espousing the authors' vision, any innovation that goes forward must be firmly anchored in two underlying assumptions, one of method and the other of paradigm.

The first assumption stems from the firm idea that any healthcare innovation project cannot start from a tabula rasa but must always sprout from the rich heritage of experience and expertise that professional bureaucracies hold.

The second assumption is related to the definition of the childbirth event in its incontrovertible natural and physiological nature, which must never be questioned even through the interpretative grids of different disciplines.

Prof. Paola Adinolfi
Director of the Interdepartmental Center for Research in Law, Economics and Management of Public Administration
University of Salerno

Prof. Antonio Mollo
Professor of Obstetrics and Gynecology, Azienda Ospedaliero Universitaria San Giovanni di Dio e Ruggi d'Aragona Scuola Medica Salernitana
University of Salerno

Acknowledgments

This work is the result of a long journey of training and research at the University of Salerno. One of the largest universities in Southern Italy, it symbolizes the universe of economic, medical, humanistic, social, scientific, and legal knowledge. Immersed in the perfect architecture of nature that surrounds the campus, our research group studies and promotes organizational, managerial, and social innovation that develops beyond the boundaries of individual disciplinary domains. To all fellow travelers, especially the faculty and researchers in the Department of Business Sciences – Management & Innovation Systems, we extend our thanks for the always lively and constructive discussions in all research projects that center around the themes of management and innovation.

Deep and special thanks go to our mentor, Prof. Paola Adinolfi, director of the Interdepartmental Center for Research in Law, Economics and Management of Public Administration and the Master's Program in Management of Healthcare Companies and Organizations (DAOSAN). To Prof. Adinolfi, we offer our most heartfelt thanks for being a source of visionary thinking applied to the world of Healthcare and of all complex organizations, for being able to grasp among the world's phenomena connections invisible to most, to succeed in abstracting new paradigms, concretizing them in innovative projects and multiplying them in a virtuous exercise of collective intelligence.

Special thanks also to Prof. Antonio Mollo, professor of Obstetrics and Gynecology at the Azienda Ospedaliero Universitaria San Giovanni di Dio e Ruggi d'Aragona Scuola Medica Salernitana, for his great ability to debate with scholars from other disciplines. Thanks to Prof. Mollo for all the times that, in the outpatient clinics of his department and in the meeting rooms of the University, he enlightened us with his clarity and profound competence on the complex miracle of birth.

A thank you multiplied by the number of pages in this text to Davide de Gennaro, a colleague in Business Organization and an extraordinary friend. The patient and tireless effort of reading and revising every word herein makes this work somewhat like his second child, after little Michele!

xiv   Acknowledgments

We remember with gratitude all the colleagues in computer science, statistics, management, law, business administration and organization who sat at the working table of the Training, Reorganizing, Evaluating, Enabling (TREE) for Natural Birth project (POR FESR CAMPANIA 2014/2020), demonstrating how a multilingual communicative register for the birth pathway could be possible.

We thank all the professionals of the Italian healthcare world who, in 16 cycles of the Master's Degree in Management of Healthcare Companies and Organizations (DAOSAN), have inspired our research on the real issues of the healthcare world, in a synergistic effort of learning community that creates value around humans. Among the many faces and minds, we recognize how the impetus for this research was provided by Dr. Ida Andreozzi, manager at the UOSD PDTA Analysis and Monitoring, LEA Governance and Appropriateness of Care – ASL Salerno; by Dr. Anna Bellissimo, Director of UPC patient safety and clinical risk management and Dr. Sara Marino, Medical Managers at the UOSD PDTA Analysis and Monitoring, – A.S.L. Salerno; and by Dr. Carmela Muccione, Director of Professionalizing Activities (DAP) of the undergraduate course in Midwifery (University of Naples - Asl Salerno). They gave the spark that ignited the engine of our study.

This work, moreover, has benefited from careful and timely discussion with Dr. Carlo Di Maio of the Department of Gynecology and Obstetrics of the Azienda Ospedaliero-Universitaria San Giovanni di Dio Ruggie d'Aragona Scuola Medica Salernitana; with Dr. Paola De Rosa, midwife at the University Hospital of Parma; and Dr. Valentina Di Cuonzo, midwife at the Asl of Lecce.

A thank you to all the women we met during their personal birth journey and to all the women who "give life."

To my father, my mother, Mimma: always and forever indispensable cardinal points in every journey of mine, personal and professional.

To Anna: an everyday example of a woman in whom the forces of nature and an absolute goodness capable of moving the world are all concentrated together.

To Antonio and Carlotta: for them any form of thanks would be too modest, for all the endless months, days, and hours in which they did without me, without making me feel lacking. This book is dedicated to them, the source and engine of my every breath.
Gabriella

To my mother and my father who have left me the greatest legacy: the roots and the wings.
To Assunta: we are each other's greatest gift from our parents.
To Maddalena e Rosario, who have filled our home with joy.
Margherita

Introduction

Pregnancy and childbirth symbolize a period of decision-making during which women feel the need to express their needs and receive correct information leading to informed choices. Over the years, the issue of the birth path has become increasingly important due to the increase in the number of deliveries performed by cesarean section, a surgical practice capable of compromising the health of the woman and the baby if performed without real medical necessity and with a strong impact on the healthcare system from the organizational, social, clinical, and economic points of view (Betran et al., 2021; World Health Organization, 2015).

In the international scenario, the choice of opting for surgery rather than favoring natural childbirth is conditioned less by the presence of real differences in the health status of the population than by multiple factors of a cultural, economic, and organizational nature, leading to increasingly inappropriate decisions from the clinical point of view (Dhakal-Rai et al., 2021; Shaterian et al., 2021). In light of the scenario described, it is believed that the multidisciplinary approach is the most suitable to analyze and hypothesize a possible redesign of the birth pathway considering the multiple aspects of complexity related to the interdependence between phases of care, the relationships between multiple actors, and the heterogeneity with which services are delivered.

This book is organized into five chapters.

The first chapter highlights a multidimensional framing of the birth event, unquestionably conceived in its physiological nature and explored in social, cultural, and technological terms (e.g., Peahl et al., 2020). The chapter provides a detailed look at the international debate aimed at promoting new organizational models that enable integration, safety, sustainability, and appropriateness of healthcare provisions.

The second chapter, starting from the paradigms of health that have characterized the health context over the years, highlights an organizational analysis of structures, actors, and relationships that move in unison with the different models of health. In particular, guided by the virtuous and predominant centrality of patient care needs, it delves into

DOI: 10.4324/9781003330097-1

the process view of healthcare organization with contextualization to the birth pathway, which sees women as the beating heart of the continuum of social and health care (e.g., Dahlen et al., 2022).

The third chapter highlights the birth pathway in organizational terms, drawing it graphically as a Value System and, in terms as objective as possible, describing it in its core processes of preconception care, access to the birth pathway, labor, delivery, and puerperium. The chapter, moreover, highlights how the crisp and linear flow of the organizational process of the birth path hides pockets of unpredictability of action and complexity of (also lean) management that let the medical dimension of childbirth prevail (e.g., Joosten et al., 2009).

The fourth chapter highlights a study conducted in the Italian context and focuses, in particular, on two survey units in southern Italy, which is considered particularly significant because of the alarmingly high and inappropriate rates of cesarean section and, therefore, the pushed medicalization of birth (Laurita Longo et al., 2020). Through the construction of a clinical and extra-clinical dataset, variables related to the mode of childbirth are analyzed and some useful determinants are identified for the redesign of the birth pathway capable of inspiring more conscious and rational choices.

The fifth chapter, in light of the multidimensional analysis conducted, highlights a proposal for redesigning the birth pathway based on a new health paradigm that sees the centrality of the couple and the engaged fatherhood approach (e.g., Grau-Grau 2021). This concluding chapter also proposes a reconfiguration of the birth pathway that moves from Value System to Value Constellation (Normann & Ramirez, 1993), by welcoming stakeholders who have not traditionally been contemplated and who are called upon not only to add value but also to reinvent it by leveraging distributed Health Literacy and Empowerment (Edwards et al., 2015; Muscat et al., 2022).

This book proposes useful implications for future research on healthcare organizations and for possible policy interventions.

First, the renewed centrality of the couple and the fatherhood approach within the birth pathway provides stimuli for further research aimed at exploring the resulting change in terms of gender roles involved in care.

Second, the renewed boundaries of the Value Constellation suggest a space for multidisciplinary and multistakeholder action and reflection, useful for both integrated policy pathways and lines of research inspired by an engaged approach that addresses real-life problems for the couple and society as a whole.

Finally, this book provides the ICT domain disciplines with the cue to develop integrated information systems that can nurture and accelerate HL and distributed empowerment while strengthening the Value Constellation's autopoietic capacity.

References

Betran, A. P., Ye, J., Moller, A. B., Souza, J. P., & Zhang, J. (2021). Trends and projections of caesarean section rates: global and regional estimates. *BMJ Global Health*, *6*(6), e005671.

Dahlen, H. G., Drandic, D., Shah, N., & Cadee, F. (2022). Supporting midwifery is the answer to the wicked problems in maternity care. *The Lancet Global Health*, *10*(7), e951–e952.

Dhakal-Rai, S., van Teijlingen, E., Regmi, P. R., Wood, J., Dangal, G., & Dhakal, K. B. (2021). Caesarean section for non-medical reasons: a rising public health issue. *Journal of Karnali Acadamy of Health Sciences*, *4*(2), 1–12.

Edwards, M., Wood, F., Davies, M., & Edwards, A. (2015). 'Distributed health literacy': longitudinal qualitative analysis of the roles of health literacy mediators and social networks of people living with a long-term health condition. *Health Expectations*, *18*(5), 1180–1193.

Grau-Grau, M., las Heras Maestro, M., & Riley Bowles, H. (2021). Engaged fatherhood for men, families and gender equality: healthcare, social policy, and work perspectives. Springer.

Joosten, T., Bongers, I., & Janssen, R. (2009). Application of lean thinking to health care: issues and observations. *International Journal for Quality in Health Care*, *21*(5), 341–347.

Laurita Longo, V., Odjidja, E. N., Beia, T. K., Neri, M., Kielmann, K., Gittardi, I., ... & Lanzone, A. (2020). "An unnecessary cut?" multilevel health systems analysis of drivers of caesarean sections rates in Italy: a systematic review. *BMC Pregnancy and Childbirth*, *20*(1), 1–16.

Muscat, D. M., Gessler, D., Ayre, J., Norgaard, O., Heuck, I. R., Haar, S., & Maindal, H. T. (2022). Seeking a deeper understanding of 'distributed health literacy': a systematic review. *Health Expectations*, *25*(3), 856–868.

Normann, R., & Ramirez, R. (1993). From value chain to value constellation: designing interactive strategy. *Harvard Business Review*, *71*(4), 65–77.

Peahl, A. F., Smith, R. D., & Moniz, M. H. (2020). Prenatal care redesign: creating flexible maternity care models through virtual care. *American Journal of Obstetrics and Gynecology*, *223*(3), 389–e1.

Shaterian, N., Rahnemaei, F. A., Ghavidel, N., & Abdi, F. (2021). Elective cesarean section on maternal request without indication: reasons for it, and its advantages and disadvantages. *Central European Journal of Nursing and Midwifery*, *12*(3), 458–469.

World Health Organization. (2015). *WHO statement on caesarean section rates* (No. WHO/RHR/15.02). World Health Organization.

1 The multidisciplinary nature of childbirth

Gabriella Piscopo and Margherita Ruberto

1.1 Defining aspects and characteristics of the birth path

In the past, the "masters of childbirth" were midwives who had learned the art from their own mothers or grandmothers (Ranisio, 2014). With only empirical knowledge and experience as a guide, they accompanied women through pregnancy, childbirth, and the early years of the child's life. Although midwives were not educated in the art of medicine, they were able to cope with all the difficulties that could arise during the course of pregnancy and sought the help of a doctor only when it was necessary to save the life of the fetus or the mother. Thus, childbirth was experienced as an intimate family event during which the centrality of the woman was valued. Today, medicalization of childbirth has led to the devaluation of women's skills regarding pregnancy and childbirth. Childbirth is often experienced as trauma. Many women are frightened of pain, seeing it as an enemy to be eliminated rather than as a guide in the difficult and unknown journey of childbirth.

In the past, pain in childbirth was considered inevitable and took on a strongly symbolic meaning. The current negative connotation of pain prompts consideration of medicalized alternative proposals, such as the increasingly widespread practice of cesarean section.

In recent years, the need to improve the quality of birth care has made it essential to develop new organizational models based on the management of the overall health care delivery process with a view to integration, safety, sustainability, and appropriateness.

The need to redesign the birth path stems from the fact that it represents a process of care characterized by fragmentation and discontinuity. Although pregnancy should not be treated as a pathology but as a physiological condition, the approach taken by health care providers is characterized by high heterogeneity due to the absence of a common and uniform pathway, with negative repercussions not only on the proper management of pregnancy but also on the organizational aspects of care activities. In fact, in most developed countries, birth care is an extremely critical area characterized by excessive use of private facilities, increasing medicalization of pregnancy and childbirth and overutilization of invasive diagnostic and therapeutic procedures. In

DOI: 10.4324/9781003330097-2

addition, there is a lack of continuity of care between territorial and hospital services and a lack of homogeneity in the provision of services.

One of the major critical issues noted within the birth path is the increase in the number of deliveries performed by cesarean section, which is one of the quality indicators most frequently used internationally by governments and public health professionals to assess progress in maternal and child health (Abdelazim et al., 2020; Betran et al., 2018; Rosa et al., 2019; Saleh et al., 2017). Cesarean section is a surgical practice that can reduce maternal and perinatal mortality and morbidity when performed based on a specific medical indication. However, like any other surgical procedure, it is not risk-free and can compromise the health of the mother and infant as well as the potential success of future pregnancies, being associated with both short- and long-term complications (Boerma et al., 2018; Keag et al., 2018; Sandall et al., 2018; Sobhy et al., 2019).

Thus, there is a need to prepare and plan the entire birth path on the basis of organizational models that allow for proper pregnancy framing in order to ensure higher levels of appropriateness, quality, and safety in order to reduce maternal, perinatal, and neonatal mortality. Despite the strong differentiation at the national level, the birth path may be an optimal model for redesigning the management and organizational logic underlying birth. Adopting this model for internal organizational protocols may, therefore, be a viable way to improve the level of care offered while acting on aspects that today negatively impact the level of perceived quality.

1.2 Social context: the social determinants and epidemiology of birth path

For health policy purposes, it is important to assess how and at what stages of life health inequalities occur. Maternal and child health problems can cause serious harm to communities, so inequalities need to be addressed even before pregnancy. Indeed, there is evidence in the literature that many inequalities in population health originate during pregnancy (Begum et al., 2017; Sharifi et al., 2018; Singh et al., 2020). Several social factors, including low levels of education, low socioeconomic status, residence in a disadvantaged area, and poor prenatal care, are associated with an increased risk of adverse pregnancy outcomes such as preterm childbirth, low childbirth weight, and neonatal and postneonatal death (Gadson et al., 2017; Manuck, 2017; Mehra et al., 2017; Taywade & Pisudde, 2017).

According to Le and Nguyen (2020), there is a positive relationship between maternal education levels and utilization of health services; in fact, low maternal education has been shown to be associated with poor utilization of prenatal services (Kim et al., 2018; Wang et al., 2021).

Kramer et al. (2000) believe that a low level of education may cause pregnant women to be less attentive to prevention and perceptions of health problems and to engage in harmful behaviors during pregnancy such as smoking or alcohol consumption. According to Overgaard et al. (2012), pregnant women living in socioeconomic disadvantage perceive themselves as having little knowledge and ability to make health-related decisions, making them more trusting of medical "experts." Thus, a higher level of education is likely to improve women's ability to communicate with health professionals and acquire basic health information about the benefits of good prenatal care and reproductive health services so as to make informed and appropriate choices. Disadvantage related to socioeconomic conditions is accompanied by disadvantage related to citizenship, where additional factors such as cultural, social, and genetic may come into play. Migrant women are often unable to benefit from health care appropriate to their needs for a variety of reasons, ranging from difficulty in accessing services, to communication problems, to the inadequacies of health care facilities to meet their cultural needs. The maternal health outcomes of most migrant women are, in fact, poorer than those of other women, with worse pregnancy and neonatal health outcomes (Heaman et al., 2013; Small et al., 2014). Other studies in the literature have examined the relationship between employment status during pregnancy and health outcomes: employment during pregnancy can expose one to a number of risks related to chemical, physical, and psycho-social agents present in the workplace and can influence pregnancy outcomes such as miscarriage, premature childbirth, and childbirth weight and can also interact with fetal development (Cai et al., 2020).

Many critical issues related to the birth path also stem from changes in the basic epidemiology of women. For example, overweight and obesity are increasing globally among women, putting them at increased risk of congenital anomalies during pregnancy (particularly neural tube and abdominal wall defects), venous thromboembolism, pre-eclampsia, gestational diabetes, postpartum hemorrhage, and increased likelihood that operative vaginal delivery or cesarean section will be required (Menting et al., 2019; Tucker et al., 2021; Wei Hu et al., 2022). There is also an increase in alcohol and tobacco use, and, as shown by data in the literature, smoking by the mother during pregnancy is associated with underweight childbirths and adverse physiological effects such as congenital heart defects and sudden infant death syndrome (Alverson et al., 2011; Cui et al., 2014; Mahmoodi et al., 2015).

At the European level, the trend in recent decades is an increase in the average age of women at childbirth from 29.7 in 2008 to 30.7 in 2017. According to EUROSTAT, on average, in the EU, women gave birth to their first child in 2020 at the age of 29.3. Notably, among member states, the lowest average age at first childbirth is in Bulgaria and Albania (26.1 years) while the highest average age is in Italy (31.2 years). Italy, despite having one of the highest life expectancies on the continent, remains among the European states where fertility and birth rates are lowest, the age of mothers highest, and the first child arrives latest. The decline in childbirths in Italy can be attributed to changes in the female population at the fertile age, conventionally set between 15 and 49. In this population group, the baby boom cohort of women born during the 1970s are coming out of the reproductive phase, while younger women are fewer and fewer in number due to the effect of the so-called baby-bust, a phase of sharp decline in fertility in the 20-year period of 1976–1995 that led to the all-time low of 1.19 children per woman in 1995.

1.3 Technological context: the tools to support the birth path

Rethinking an effective and efficient birth path also involves a different assessment of the role of technologies and all digital tools that become powerful means not only of reducing costs, time, and resources but also of improving the quality of care, promoting health literacy and increasing empowerment (see Agrawal & Prabakaran, 2020; Golinelli et al., 2020; Wang et al., 2021). Technologies, in other words, enable the consolidation of women's decision-making by promoting an informed choice of mode of delivery (Sanders & Crozier, 2018).

The increasing use of technologies has radically changed the way health is managed, delivered, and measured by completely altering the role played by the patient (Feldman et al., 2018). In essence, they give rise to a comprehensive overhaul of processes in all their components.

New technologies, particularly digital technologies, now play a key role in innovating the birth path, because they represent useful tools to support both health professionals and expectant mothers. For the latter, pregnancy can be seen as a particularly powerful "formative moment" during which they are ready to change certain habits to improve their own health and that of the fetus (Mitchell & Kan, 2019). Today, pregnant women use a variety of online applications that can serve as key tools for improving empowerment, especially in terms of health management (Hughson et al., 2018; Wang et al., 2019).

Almunawar et al. (2015) identified three perspectives of empowerment: personal, medical, and social (HajiPour et al., 2016). The personal perspective is about promoting and improving the user's ability to identify his or her needs; the medical perspective is about integration between the user and the health care provider; and the social perspective involves sharing stories and experiences among users and networking between patients and health care providers. Most authors studying the empowerment phenomenon agree that effective empowerment can be achieved through active patient participation in decision-making, a high level of self-efficacy, an appropriate level of health literacy, and the creation of an enabling environment (Castro et al., 2016; Cerezo et al., 2016; Nieuwenhuijze & Leahy-Warren, 2019; Nkhoma et al., 2020).

Involvement in decision-making is especially important in pregnant women because they have to make completely new health-related decisions

(Doherty et al., 2018; Ngo et al., 2020). Although most women ask their health care providers for information, many use the Internet either because they feel that the information they receive from their doctor is unclear or to reinforce their current knowledge (Sandborg et al., 2021).

The use of a smartphone app represents an innovative approach to improving adherence and patient behavior; as confirmed by several studies in the literature, the use of these tools has been found to be effective for smoking cessation, medication adherence, and blood pressure management (Morawski et al., 2018; Musgrave et al., 2020). The use of apps can be useful to make up for limited information sharing about different moments of the childbirth journey, including that of childbirth, which is of greatest concern to expectant mothers. As is well known, to overcome this fear, the use of cesarean section is often considered as the optimal solution (Tripp et al., 2014).

Over the years, improvements in surgical technologies have generated the belief that cesarean section is risk-free, while data from the medical literature suggest that the procedure is associated with women's health risks that increase with multiple cesarean sections (Donati et al., 2018, 2021). Such information is not known to expectant mothers who opt for this intervention (Fenwick et al., 2010), and in this regard, technology and modern communication methods can be helpful in making up for this lack of information. Furthermore, pregnancy apps can be a useful tool for sharing information with health care providers.

Mobile apps play a key role in the delivery of educational content because they provide behavior modification tools through simple and inexpensive interventions.

In particular, the great advantage of using Internet-based (eHealth) and smartphone (mHealth) information sources is related to the promotion of maternal health literacy through the presence of information on prevention and health promotion and health services (Iyawa et al., 2020; Maier. et al., 2021).

Sometimes, the information sought online aims to compensate for the poor interaction between patients and health care providers, who are sometimes unable to guide and support the mother-to-be in her choices due to ineffective and unempathetic communication. According to research conducted by Kraschnewski et al. (2014), many women feel that clinic visit times are too short, that the first visit occurs too late, and that there are too few visits at the beginning of pregnancy, a time when women most need to receive more information. In other cases, women perceive health facilities as not patient-centered (Bergman & Connaughton, 2013; Nobili et al., 2007), so they prefer to use technology to bridge the information gap as they are not satisfied with the way information is provided during visits. Furthermore, although health professionals encourage women to adopt healthy behaviors during pregnancy, several authors argue that only few women receive specific and personalized recommendations (Goetz et al., 2017; Whitaker et al.,

2016). Pregnant women, mainly in industrialized countries, often use the Internet, social media and smartphone applications ("apps") to search for health information on a wide range of obstetric and pediatric topics and to share their experiences with other mothers-to-be (Frid et al., 2021; Jacobs et al., 2019; Javanmardi et al., 2018). According to several studies in the literature, apps have been found to have exciting potential to affect women's behavior during pregnancy such as monitoring maternal weight or breastfeeding (Chan & Chen, 2019; Musgrave et al., 2020). Such apps are an excellent tool for tracking women's behaviors by stimulating feedback and self-management, monitoring pregnancy development, and identifying potential risks. There are more apps for pregnancy than for any other medical topic; some have been developed, for example, to support and educate pregnant women with certain conditions such as diabetes, while others have been developed to improve diet, track and improve physical activity, monitor blood pressure, maintain a healthy weight, and help with smoking cessation. Specifically, there are four types of pregnancy apps, discussed below, which differ from each other based on the function they perform (Brown et al., 2019; Sampat et al., 2020; Tripp et al., 2014).

1. Informational apps allow the sharing of information about pregnancy and, in some cases, represent an agenda that is useful in providing guidance on accommodations to turn to if needed. The main information found in such apps concerns clinical and diagnostic tests to be performed, information on diet, recommended foods and exercise, and/or pregnancy massage tutorials.
2. Interactive apps represent the most popular category of apps, as they allow data entry and offer appropriate and specific information in addition to being customizable. These apps include personalized information and images, illustrations of the baby's growth status, and ultrasound images.
3. Instrumental apps include monitoring and calculation apps. The former are used for estimating certain values such as the expected date of delivery, fetal weight, and the record of contractions, while the latter have the main function of helping women keep track of certain parameters, such as weight gain and fetal monitoring.
4. Social networking apps allow women to share emotions and concerns about their health status with other mothers-to-be. Such apps are characterized by the presence of communities or forums that allow users to participate in discussions on particular topics.

In light of the above, there is a need for additional support to assist patients in receiving accurate information regarding both general recommendations related to the entire period of pregnancy and specific, personalized recommendations. Such support can be provided through the use of specific apps that are a useful tool for disseminating information, monitoring behavior, and improving communication between patients and health care providers.

1.4 The multidisciplinary debate in the international scenario

Globally, the childbirth phenomenon shows substantial differences in terms of caregivers involved, health services offered, and adverse outcomes such as maternal and neonatal death. According to estimates by the United Nations Inter-Agency Group for Child Mortality Estimation (IGME), the network of United Nations agencies led by UNICEF and the World Health Organization, in 2018 more than 290,000 women worldwide (an average of 800 per day) died from complications related to pregnancy or childbirth, 2.7 million babies died during the first 28 days of life, and 2.6 million babies were stillborn. Most maternal deaths occur in developing countries where many deliveries still occur at home, but without the assistance of skilled and trained personnel to manage obstetric complications (Graham et al., 2001; Ozimek & Kilpatrick, 2018; Sundari, 2020). This generates concern regarding the high maternal mortality in these countries, as women who develop life-threatening complications during pregnancy and delivery require appropriate and accessible care (Wondie, 2021). In such countries, hemorrhage is the leading cause of maternal death, while in developed countries, most deaths are due to other causes, mainly related to complications of anesthesia and cesarean section (Gulumser et al., 2019; Mekonnen & Gebremariam, 2018). Many deaths could be avoided if skilled care capable of early recognition of treatment of complications with timely referral to hospitals for more complex care were provided. In recent years, in developing countries, several efforts have been made to strengthen health systems to support maternal and child health services including expanding the network of health facilities, resulting in improved access, increasing the workforce in order to meet growing demand, and reducing financial barriers to access to improve care delivery and quality of care (Black et al., 2017; Lowdermilk et al., 2019; Michel-Schuldt et al., 2020). In contrast, in most developed countries, pregnancies are planned, complications are few, and outcomes are generally favorable for both mother and baby, but there has been an increase in the use of cesarean section, often for nonmedical indications (O'donovan & O'donovan, 2018). It is evident, therefore, that it is necessary to contextualize the differences between countries in terms of social, cultural, and economic factors as well as the present health care model.

Wagner (2001) classified birthing care models into three categories:

1 highly medicalized, "high-tech" model, based on high technology and low involvement of midwives in the care pathway. This model can be

found in the United States, Ireland, Russia, the Czech Republic, France, Belgium, and urban areas of Brazil;
2   less medicalized model, characterized by greater involvement of midwives and low use of interventions. This model is found in the Netherlands and Scandinavian countries;
3   intermediate model, found in Britain, Canada, Germany, Italy, and Japan. In these countries, birth care appears to be overly medicalized in contrast to national and international guidelines that increasingly recognize its natural dimension.

Global efforts have been directed at reducing maternal and neonatal mortality by focusing on addressing the risks associated with pregnancy and childbirth. This has been the approach taken by high-income countries, where many women have access to antenatal and postnatal care that includes home visits by midwives and health workers. In most of these countries, women give childbirth in hospitals, while home childbirths are exceedingly rare. Women on a high-risk pregnancy pathway are well cared for in these facilities, as they are high-tech facilities where rapid access to interventions is allowed. In contrast, these same facilities may not be optimized for women with low-risk pregnancies. This leads to the use of excessive and inappropriate interventions resulting in prohibitive costs. In order to optimize care for low-risk pregnancy and increase satisfaction levels, delivery units run entirely by midwives have been established in some countries (see Bogren et al., 2022; Mattison et al., 2020; Walsh et al., 2020), while, in other settings, home childbirth services provided by licensed midwives are provided (Comeau et al., 2018; Ross et al., 2022).

There is a need for different models of childbirth care to continue to be explored and evaluated in terms of their ability to place the woman at the center of the care process, supporting her through the physiological journey while reducing inappropriate interventions.

References

Abdelazim, I., Alanwar, A., Shikanova, S., Kanshaiym, S., Farghali, M., Mohamed, M., ... & Karimova, B. (2020). Complications associated with higher order compared to lower order cesarean sections. *The Journal of Maternal-Fetal & Neonatal Medicine*, *33*(14), 2395–2402.

Agrawal, R., & Prabakaran, S. (2020). Big data in digital healthcare: lessons learnt and recommendations for general practice. *Heredity*, *124*(4), 525–534.

Almunawar, M. N., Anshari, M., & Younis, M. Z. (2015). Incorporating customer empowerment in mobile health. *Health Policy and Technology*, *4*(4), 312–319.

Alverson, C. J., Strickland, M. J., Gilboa, S. M., & Correa, A. (2011). Maternal smoking and congenital heart defects in the Baltimore-Washington Infant Study. *Pediatrics*, *127*(3), e647–e653.

Begum, T., Rahman, A., Nababan, H., Hoque, D. M. E., Khan, A. F., Ali, T., & Anwar, I. (2017). Indications and determinants of caesarean section delivery: evidence from a population-based study in Matlab, Bangladesh. *PloS one*, *12*(11), e0188074.

Bergman, A. A., & Connaughton, S. L. (2013). What is patient-centered care really? Voices of Hispanic prenatal patients. *Health Communication*, *28*(8), 789–799.

Betran, A. P., Temmerman, M., Kingdon, C., Mohiddin, A., Opiyo, N., Torloni, M. R., ... & Downe, S. (2018). Interventions to reduce unnecessary caesarean sections in healthy women and babies. *The Lancet*, *392*(10155), 1358–1368.

Black, R. E., Taylor, C. E., Arole, S., Bang, A., Bhutta, Z. A., Chowdhury, A. M. R., ... & Perry, H. B.. (2017). Comprehensive review of the evidence regarding the effectiveness of community–based primary health care in improving maternal, neonatal and child health: 8. summary and recommendations of the Expert Panel. *Journal of global health*, *7*(1).

Boerma, T., Ronsmans, C., Melesse, D. Y., Barros, A. J., Barros, F. C., Juan, L., ... & Temmerman, M. (2018). Global epidemiology of use of and disparities in caesarean sections. *The Lancet*, *392*(10155), 1341–1348.

Bogren, M., Jha, P., Sharma, B., & Erlandsson, K. (2022). Contextual factors influencing the implementation of midwifery-led care units in India. *Women and Birth*. (article in press).

Brown, H. M., Bucher, T., Collins, C. E., & Rollo, M. E. (2019). A review of pregnancy iPhone apps assessing their quality, inclusion of behaviour change techniques, and nutrition information. *Maternal & child nutrition*, *15*(3), e12768.

Cai, C., Vandermeer, B., Khurana, R., Nerenberg, K., Featherstone, R., Sebastianski, M., & Davenport, M. H. (2020). The impact of occupational activities during pregnancy on pregnancy outcomes: a systematic review and metaanalysis. *American Journal of Obstetrics and Gynecology*, *222*(3), 224–238.

Castro, E. M., Van Regenmortel, T., Vanhaecht, K., Sermeus, W., & Van Hecke, A. (2016). Patient empowerment, patient participation and patient-centeredness in hospital care: a concept analysis based on a literature review. *Patient education and counseling*, *99*(12), 1923–1939.

Cerezo, P. G., Juvé-Udina, M. E., & Delgado-Hito, P. (2016). Concepts and measures of patient empowerment: a comprehensive review. *Revista da Escola de Enfermagem da USP*, *50*, 0667–0674.

Chan, K. L., & Chen, M. (2019). Effects of social media and mobile health apps on pregnancy care: meta-analysis. *JMIR mHealth and uHealth*, *7*(1), e11836.

Comeau, A., Hutton, E. K., Simioni, J., Anvari, E., Bowen, M., Kruegar, S., & Darling, E. K. (2018). Home birth integration into the health care systems of eleven international jurisdictions. *Birth*, *45*(3), 311–321.

Cui, Y., Shooshtari, S., Forget, E. L., Clara, I., & Cheung, K. F. (2014). Smoking during pregnancy: findings from the 2009–2010 Canadian Community Health Survey. *PloS One*, *9*(1), e84640

Doherty, K., Barry, M., Marcano-Belisario, J., Arnaud, B., Morrison, C., Car, J., & Doherty, G. (2018). A mobile app for the self-report of psychological well-being during pregnancy (BrightSelf): qualitative design study. *JMIR Mental Health*, *5*(4), e10007

Donati, S., Fano, V., Maraschini, A., & Regional Obstetric Surveillance System Working Group. (2021). Uterine rupture: Results from a prospective population-based study in Italy. *European Journal of Obstetrics & Gynecology and Reproductive Biology*, *264*, 70–75.

Donati, S., Maraschini, A., Lega, I., D'Aloja, P., Buoncristiano, M., Manno, V., ... & Voller, F. (2018). Maternal mortality in Italy: results and perspectives of record-linkage analysis. *Acta Obstetricia et Gynecologica Scandinavica*, 97(11), 1317–1324.

Feldman, S. S., Buchalter, S., & Hayes, L. W. (2018). Health information technology in healthcare quality and patient safety: literature review. *JMIR Medical Informatics*, 6(2), e10264.

Fenwick, J., Staff, L., Gamble, J., Creedy, D. K., & Bayes, S. (2010). Why do women request caesarean section in a normal, healthy first pregnancy?. *Midwifery*, 26(4), 394–400.

Frid, G., Bogaert, K., & Chen, K. T. (2021). Mobile Health apps for pregnant women: systematic search, evaluation, and analysis of features. *Journal of Medical Internet Research*, 23(10), e25667.

Gadson, A., Akpovi, E., & Mehta, P. K. (2017). Exploring the social determinants of racial/ethnic disparities in prenatal care utilization and maternal outcome. In *Seminars in Perinatology* (Vol. 41, No. 5, pp. 308–317). WB Saunders.

Goetz, M., Müller, M., Matthies, L. M., Hansen, J., Doster, A., Szabo, A., ... & Wallwiener, S. (2017). Perceptions of patient engagement applications during pregnancy: a qualitative assessment of the patient's perspective. *JMIR mHealth and uHealth*, 5(5), e7040.

Golinelli, D., Boetto, E., Carullo, G., Nuzzolese, A. G., Landini, M. P., & Fantini, M. P. (2020). Adoption of digital technologies in health care during the COVID-19 pandemic: systematic review of early scientific literature. *Journal of Medical Internet Research*, 22(11), e22280.

Graham, W. J., Bell, J. S., & Bullough, C. H. (2001). Can skilled attendance at delivery reduce maternal mortality in developing countries?. In: *Safe motherhood strategies: a review of the evidence* (eds. De Brouwere,V.; Van Lerberghe,W.), Studies in Health Services Organisation and Policy, 17.

Gulumser, C., Engin-Ustun, Y., Keskin, L., Celen, S., Sanisoglu, S., Karaahmetoglu, S., ... & Sencan, I. (2019). Maternal mortality due to hemorrhage: population-based study in Turkey. *The Journal of Maternal-Fetal & Neonatal Medicine*, 32(23), 3998–4004.

HajiPour, L., Hosseini Tabaghdehi, M., TaghiZoghi, Z., & Behzadi, Z. (2016). Empowerment of pregnant women. *Journal of Holistic Nursing and Midwifery*, 26(3), 16–24.

Heaman, M., Bayrampour, H., Kingston, D., Blondel, B., Gissler, M., Roth, C., ... & Gagnon, A. (2013). Migrant women's utilization of prenatal care: a systematic review. *Maternal and Child Health Journal*, 17(5), 816–836.

Hughson, J. A. P., Daly, J. O., Woodward-Kron, R., Hajek, J., & Story, D. (2018). The rise of pregnancy apps and the implications for culturally and linguistically diverse women: narrative review. *JMIR mHealth and uHealth*, 6(11), e9119.

Iyawa, G. E., Langan-Martin, J., Sevalie, S., & Masikara, W. (2020). mHealth as tools for development in mental health. In *Impacts of Information Technology on Patient Care and Empowerment* (pp. 58–80). IGI Global.

Jacobs, E. J., van Steijn, M. E., & van Pampus, M. G. (2019). Internet usage of women attempting pregnancy and pregnant women in the Netherlands. *Sexual & Reproductive Healthcare*, 21, 9–14.

Javanmardi, M., Noroozi, M., Mostafavi, F., & Ashrafi-Rizi, H. (2018). Internet usage among pregnant women for seeking health information: a review article. *Iranian Journal of Nursing and Midwifery Research*, 23(2), 79.

Keag, O. E., Norman, J. E., & Stock, S. J. (2018). Long-term risks and benefits associated with cesarean delivery for mother, baby, and subsequent pregnancies: systematic review and meta-analysis. *PLoS Medicine, 15*(1), e1002494.

Kim, M. K., Lee, S. M., Bae, S. H., Kim, H. J., Lim, N. G., Yoon, S. J., ... & Jo, M. W. (2018). Socioeconomic status can affect pregnancy outcomes and complications, even with a universal healthcare system. *International Journal for Equity in Health, 17*(1), 1–8.

Kramer, M. S., Séguin, L., Lydon, J., & Goulet, L. (2000). Socio-economic disparities in pregnancy outcome: why do the poor fare so poorly? *Paediatric and Perinatal Epidemiology, 14*(3), 194–210.

Kraschnewski, J. L., Chuang, C. H., Poole, E. S., Peyton, T., Blubaugh, I., Pauli, J., ... & Reddy, M. (2014). Paging "Dr. Google": does technology fill the gap created by the prenatal care visit structure? Qualitative focus group study with pregnant women. *Journal of Medical Internet Research, 16*(6), e3385.

Le, K., & Nguyen, M. (2020). Shedding light on maternal education and child health in developing countries. *World Development, 133*, 105005.

Lowdermilk, D. L., Cashion, M. C., Perry, S. E., Alden, K. R., & Olshansky, E. (2019). *Maternity and Women's Health Care E-Book*. Elsevier Health Sciences.

Mahmoodi, Z., Karimlou, M., Sajjadi, H., Dejman, M., Vameghi, M., & Dolatian, M. (2015). Stressful life events and Low birth Weight: according to social determinant of health approach. *Advances in Nursing & Midwifery, 25*(90), 17–26.

Maier, E., Reimer, U., & Wickramasinghe, N. (2021). Digital healthcare services. *Electronic Markets, 31*(4), 743–746.

Manuck, T. A. (2017). Racial and ethnic differences in preterm birth: a complex, multifactorial problem. In *Seminars in perinatology* (Vol. 41, No. 8, pp. 511–518). WB Saunders.

Mattison, C. A., Lavis, J. N., Hutton, E. K., Dion, M. L., & Wilson, M. G. (2020). Understanding the conditions that influence the roles of midwives in Ontario, Canada's health system: an embedded single-case study. *BMC Health Services Research, 20*(1), 1–15.

Mehra, R., Boyd, L. M., & Ickovics, J. R. (2017). Racial residential segregation and adverse birth outcomes: a systematic review and meta-analysis. *Social Science & Medicine, 191*, 237–250.

Mekonnen, W., & Gebremariam, A. (2018). Causes of maternal death in Ethiopia between 1990 and 2016: systematic review with meta-analysis. *Ethiopian Journal of Health Development, 32*(4).

Menting, M. D., Mintjens, S., van de Beek, C., Frick, C. J., Ozanne, S. E., Limpens, J., ... & Painter, R. C.. (2019). Maternal obesity in pregnancy impacts offspring cardiometabolic health: Systematic review and meta-analysis of animal studies. *Obesity Reviews, 20*(5), 675–685.

Michel-Schuldt, M., McFadden, A., Renfrew, M., & Homer, C. (2020). The provision of midwife-led care in low-and middle-income countries: an integrative review. *Midwifery, 84*, 102659.

Mitchell, M., & Kan, L. (2019). Digital technology and the future of health systems. *Health Systems & Reform, 5*(2), 113–120.

Morawski, K., Ghazinouri, R., Krumme, A., Lauffenburger, J. C., Lu, Z., Durfee, E., ... & Choudhry, N. K. (2018). Association of a smartphone application with medication adherence and blood pressure control: the MedISAFE-BP randomized clinical trial. *JAMA Internal Medicine, 178*(6), 802–809.

Musgrave, L. M., Kizirian, N. V., Homer, C. S., & Gordon, A. (2020). Mobile phone apps in Australia for improving pregnancy outcomes: systematic search on app stores. *JMIR mHealth and uHealth*, *8*(11), e22340.

Ngo, E., Truong, M. B. T., & Nordeng, H. (2020). Use of decision support tools to empower pregnant women: systematic review. *Journal of Medical Internet Research*, *22*(9), e19436.

Nieuwenhuijze, M., & Leahy-Warren, P. (2019). Women's empowerment in pregnancy and childbirth: a concept analysis. *Midwifery*, *78*, 1–7.

Nkhoma, D. E., Lin, C. P., Katengeza, H. L., Soko, C. J., Estinfort, W., Wang, Y. C., ... & Iqbal, U. (2020). Girls' empowerment and adolescent pregnancy: a systematic review. *International Journal of Environmental Research and Public Health*, *17*(5), 1664.

Nobili, M. P., Piergrossi, S., Brusati, V., & Moja, E. A. (2007). The effect of patient-centered contraceptive counseling in women who undergo a voluntary termination of pregnancy. *Patient Education and Counseling*, *65*(3), 361–368.

O'donovan, C., & O'donovan, J. (2018). Why do women request an elective cesarean delivery for non-medical reasons? A systematic review of the qualitative literature. *Birth*, *45*(2), 109–119.

Overgaard, C., Fenger-Grøn, M., & Sandall, J. (2012). Freestanding midwifery units versus obstetric units: does the effect of place of birth differ with level of social disadvantage? *BMC Public Health*, *12*(1), 1–14.

Ozimek, J. A., & Kilpatrick, S. J. (2018). Maternal mortality in the twenty-first century. *Obstetrics and Gynecology Clinics*, *45*(2), 175–186.

Ranisio, G. (2014). Il percorso nascita: dalle medicine popolari a "Le culture del parto"(1985). *AM. Rivista della Società Italiana di Antropologia Medica*, *16*(38).

Rosa, F., Perugin, G., Schettini, D., Romano, N., Romeo, S., Podestà, R., ... & Gandolfo, N. (2019). Imaging findings of cesarean delivery complications: cesarean scar disease and much more. *Insights into imaging*, *10*(1), 1–14.

Ross, L., Jolles, D., Hoehn-Velasco, L., Wright, J., Bauer, K., & Stapleton, S. (2022). Salary and Workload of Midwives Across Birth Center Practice Types and State Regulatory Structures. *Journal of Midwifery & Women's Health*, *67*(2), 244–250.

Saleh, A. M., Dudenhausen, J. W., & Ahmed, B. (2017). Increased rates of cesarean sections and large families: a potentially dangerous combination. *Journal of Perinatal Medicine*, *45*(5), 517–521.

Sampat, B., Sharma, A., & Prabhakar, B. (2020). Understanding Factors Influencing the Usage Intention of Mobile Pregnancy Applications. In *International Working Conference on Transfer and Diffusion of IT* (pp. 641–654). Springer, Cham.

Sandall, J., Tribe, R. M., Avery, L., Mola, G., Visser, G. H., Homer, C. S., ... & Temmerman, M. (2018). Short-term and long-term effects of caesarean section on the health of women and children. *The Lancet*, *392*(10155), 1349–1357.

Sandborg, J., Henriksson, P., Larsen, E., Lindqvist, A. K., Rutberg, S., Söderström, E., ... & Löf, M. (2021). Participants' engagement and satisfaction with a smartphone app intended to support healthy weight gain, diet, and physical activity during pregnancy: qualitative study within the HealthyMoms trial. *JMIR mHealth and uHealth*, *9*(3), e26159.

Sanders, R. A., & Crozier, K. (2018). How do informal information sources influence women's decision-making for birth? A meta-synthesis of qualitative studies. *BMC pregnancy and childbirth*, *18*(1), 1–26.

Sharifi, N., Dolatian, M., Kazemi, A. F. N., & Pakzad, R. (2018). The relationship between the social determinants of health and preterm birth in Iran based on the who model: a systematic review and meta-analysis. *International Journal of Womens Health and Reproduction Sciences*, *6*(2), 10.

Singh, N., Pradeep, Y., & Jauhari, S. (2020). Indications and determinants of cesarean section: a cross-sectional study. *International Journal of Applied and Basic Medical Research*, *10*(4), 280.

Small, R., Roth, C., Raval, M., Shafiei, T., Korfker, D., Heaman, M., ... & Gagnon, A. (2014). Immigrant and non-immigrant women's experiences of maternity care: a systematic and comparative review of studies in five countries. *BMC Pregnancy and Childbirth*, *14*(1), 1–17.

Sobhy, S., Arroyo-Manzano, D., Murugesu, N., Karthikeyan, G., Kumar, V., Kaur, I., ... & Thangaratinam, S. (2019). Maternal and perinatal mortality and complications associated with caesarean section in low-income and middle-income countries: a systematic review and meta-analysis. *The Lancet*, *393*(10184), 1973–1982.

Sundari, T. K. (2020). *The untold story: how the health care systems in developing countries contribute to maternal mortality* (pp. 173–190). Routledge.

Taywade, M. L., & Pisudde, P. M. (2017). Study of sociodemographic determinants of low birth weight in Wardha district, India. *Clinical Epidemiology and Global Health*, *5*(1), 14–20.

Tripp, N., Hainey, K., Liu, A., Poulton, A., Peek, M., Kim, J., & Nanan, R. (2014). An emerging model of maternity care: smartphone, midwife, doctor?. *Women and Birth*, *27*(1), 64–67.

Tucker, A. R., Brown, H. L., & Dotters-Katz, S. K. (2021). Maternal weight gain and infant birth weight in women with class III obesity. *American Journal of Perinatology*, *38*(08), 816–820.

Wagner, M. (2001). Fish can't see water: the need to humanize birth. *International Journal of Gynecology & Obstetrics*, *75*, S25–S37.

Walsh, D., Spiby, H., McCourt, C., Coleby, D., Grigg, C., Bishop, S., ... & Thornton, J. (2020). Factors influencing utilisation of 'free-standing' and 'alongside' midwifery units for low-risk births in England: a mixed-methods study. *Health Services and Delivery Research*, *8*(12).

Wang, N., Deng, Z., Wen, L. M., Ding, Y., & He, G. (2019). Understanding the use of smartphone apps for health information among pregnant Chinese women: mixed methods study. *JMIR mHealth and uHealth*, *7*(6), e12631.

Wang, H., Frasco, E., Takesue, R., & Tang, K. (2021). Maternal education level and maternal healthcare utilization in the Democratic Republic of the Congo: an analysis of the multiple indicator cluster survey 2017/18. *BMC Health Services Research*, *21*(1), 1–13.

Wang, Q., Su, M., Zhang, M., & Li, R. (2021). Integrating digital technologies and public health to fight Covid-19 pandemic: key technologies, applications, challenges and outlook of digital healthcare. *International Journal of Environmental Research and Public Health*, *18*(11), 6053.

Wei, X., Hu, J., Liu, Y., Ma, Y., & Wen, D. (2022). Association between marginally low birth weight and obesity-related outcomes and indirect effects via attention-deficit hyperactivity disorder and abnormal eating. *Obesity Facts*, *15*(2), 197–208.

Whitaker, K. M., Wilcox, S., Liu, J., Blair, S. N., & Pate, R. R. (2016). Provider advice and women's intentions to meet weight gain, physical activity, and nutrition guidelines during pregnancy. *Maternal and Child Health Journal*, *20*(11), 2309–2317.

Wondie, A. G. (2021). The association between unmet need for contraception and unintended pregnancy among reproductive-age women in Ethiopia. *Medicine Access@ Point of Care*, *5*, 23992026211033436.

2 The managerial and organizational perspective of healthcare

Gabriella Piscopo

2.1 Management profiles in healthcare: health paradigms and institutional approaches

Healthcare organizations are characterized by certain organizational and managerial identifying elements. Key dimensions include the high professionalism of the actors and the extreme complexity of action related to the variety, variability, and unpredictability of internal and external phenomena (see Kunz & Oxman, 1998; Monrouxe & Rees, 2017; Sculpher et al., 2004).

2.1.1 Complexity and variability of healthcare

Over the years, the dimension of complexity has taken on a particularly acute emphasis (Churruca et al., 2019; Kannampallil et al., 2011; Rouse & Serban, 2014). This phenomenon is related not only to the variety of new care needs and the evolution of diseases but also to the progressive bureaucratization of work processes, the growing dissatisfaction of patients with the quality of healthcare services, and the emergence of sharp health inequalities. Moreover, the spread of new technologies has introduced an additional critical element related to the number of stakeholders involved in diagnosis and treatment pathways (e.g., Geampana & Perrotta, 2022). Technology, in turn, has led to the creation of new relationships and channels through which different actors interact (Spena & Cristina, 2019). The combined action of these factors imposes a continuous rethinking regarding the way health services are delivered, with a constant tension to find solutions that are valid and appropriate in therapeutic terms and, at the same time, sustainable in financial terms.

The dimension of variability in the health sector comes in different guises and can take on different meanings depending on the specific context in which it operates (see Pimentel et al., 2021). While organizational variability can be traced to the way in which services are delivered by healthcare facilities for patient management and the definition of care pathways, professional variability can be more directly traced to professional choices, skills, and behaviors. Clinical activities are, in fact, unlikely to be standardized, because they are particularly susceptible to the actions and knowledge of individual professionals. For a professional, multiple decisions and behaviors are possible with regard to the same patient; similarly, multiple fates of care are possible for the same patient (e.g., Carlini et al., 2022; Harrison et al., 2017). It also frequently occurs that, in the process of diagnosis and treatment of a health problem, multiple professionals from the same discipline, multiple disciplines, multiple organizational units, and multiple organizations are involved in the path of social-health relations. Specifically, the care pathway that the patient follows through the healthcare system crosses three functional cycles: the medical cycle, consisting of the traditional phases of history, diagnosis, treatment, and follow-up; the care and custodial cycle, which includes nursing and patient support activities; and the administrative cycle, which concerns the management of economic-financial and legal processes (see Abraham & Moretz, 2012; Joshi et al., 2014; Nguyen & Nagase, 2021). The traditional cultural distance between the different cycles is made even more acute within the medical cycle, characterized, in recent years, by the increase in professional specializations (Babiker et al., 2014). While this ensures the effectiveness of the provision, from the organizational point of view there is a resulting strong need for coordination and composition of fragmentation as a counterbalance (Miller & Hubley, 2017).

The highlighted dynamic of complex functioning, together with its perennial evolutionary motion, makes the healthcare context a particularly challenging field of study and experimentation for management studies and even more fascinating for organizational science. Organizational design choices, in fact, have long been guided by the bureaucratic logic typical of the Public Administration paradigm (see Costa Oliveira et al., 2021), which has held little regard for the importance of good design fit. With a somewhat utopian vision, the central state has been given the responsibility for vertically managing the care system by adopting homogeneous organizational models across countries. Uniform management criteria and the adoption of the rigid principle of command and control, however, proved jarring in light of the extreme variety of organizational entities that make up the healthcare system (e.g., Anttonen et al., 2012).

2.1.2 Healthcare reforms and myths

The turning point, marking a real paradigm shift, is represented by the healthcare reform born in the Anglo-Saxon context and promulgating the principles of universality, equity, and ethicality. The Anglo-Saxon example serves as a stimulus for other national systems in promoting appropriate management of resources in healthcare (Simonet, 2015). The idea is also gaining ground that the managerial approach to healthcare management is the ideal solution to overcome the limitations of the publicist approach. The New Public Management (NPM) paradigm was born (Barzelay, 2001), which aspires to study and manage public organizations in a new way (Gow & Dufour, 2000; O'Flynn, 2007), following the example of what has already been experienced in the private sector.

Although the evolving scholarly debate has seen NPM take on different definitions and applications within different national contexts (Hall et al., 2015; Leicht et al., 2009), it is possible to recognize certain underlying assumptions defined by Adinolfi (Adinolfi 2004) myths. Significantly, the myths of universalism, monocentrism, rationalism, technicalism, and organizational individualism transversally accommodate all NPM experiences that have manifested within the international context.

The universalism myth tends to recognize in private sector managerial principles the dream of "one best way" (Bradby et al., 2020) – that is, the solution formula for all problems that plague public organizations. However, the weak links that dominate among different organizations in the healthcare context blatantly debunk this myth by concretely demonstrating the impossibility of a single approach coping with extremely diverse scenarios on the intra- and inter-organizational level.

Monocentrism stems from the idea of the state with a predominant role (Byrkjeflot, 2005), which makes prevalent use of strategic planning logic. Again, the health sector disproves the value of this myth by demonstrating that real value for the organization does not come from perfectly designed plans that are difficult to translate into practice but, rather, from the ability to activate all the energies diffused within the organization and to artfully orchestrate its competencies.

The rationalistic myth anchors its vision to the utopia of being able to measure any phenomenon within organizations. The resulting concept of organizational effectiveness, however, is poorly reconciled with the dynamic nature of healthcare organizations, which are constantly projected not only to achieve the goals set by plans and programs but also to activate a continuous process of learning and innovation.

The myth of technicism is closely linked to the idea of the technical and complex nature of public administration problems, solvable only through technical expertise that can be little influenced by politics (Jun, 2007). Indeed, in the field of healthcare, the debate on the strong admixture between politicians and technicians is particularly lively. The former, in fact, exert their influence on bureaucrats so that they pursue the goals formulated on the political level. At the same time, bureaucrats strive to receive legitimacy from politics in order to earn a satisfactory career prospect (Adinolfi & Borgonovi, 2018).

The myth of organizational individualism is based on the desirability and possibility of breaking down the public sector into its elementary parts in order to increase its efficiency, effectiveness and cost-effectiveness. This myth, more than any other, has influenced the organizational dynamics of the healthcare context by determining the design of models inspired by the intra-organizational vision (Koelewijn et al., 2012; Lukas et al., 2007), oriented toward efficiency and the clear identification of responsibilities along the vertical line. The application of such organizational models has resulted in an extreme decomposition of services that has caused the value to be lost from the holistic view of care. Moreover, the exclusive focus on hierarchical control and the clear distribution of authority and responsibility tend to neglect the system perspective altogether, losing sight of the inter-organizational spillovers and effects.

Underlying the typical NPM organizational model is the bio-medical paradigm of health, focusing exclusively on the treatment of health problem and not on broader health prevention and promotion (see Andrews et al., 2019; Noblet & Rodwell, 2009).

A more mature view of health services is associated with the later New Public Governance (Osborne, 2006) approach, which, overcoming the centralist view of the state, recognizes the pluralistic nature of the health system—that is, the composite and heterogeneous nature of different actors with distinctive tasks and responsibilities (Dickinson, 2016; Tenbensel et al., 2021). New Public Governance can also be represented through four dominant myths: polycentrism, polyrationality, a focus on the organizational dimension, and a focus on social and extra-economic values (Adinolfi 2004). These myths provide a useful lens to observe the evolutionary dynamics in the healthcare context. In particular, this lens allows us to investigate the roots of the new paradigm of health, which, going beyond the bio-medical approach, assumes the boundaries of a bio-psyco-social model aimed at promoting and improving conditions of well-being.

The myth of polycentrism dismantles the idea of the central state unilaterally controlling social processes. This monolithic vision is replaced by that of the inert-organizational network in which institutions and civil society actors operate. The state abandons the role of centrally located manager to assume that of orchestrator of value generated within inter-organizational networks. Associated with this new vision is the myth of polyrationality, for which there is a shared responsibility for health outcomes resulting from synergistic interaction between public and private actors.

The myth of the inter-organizational dimension complements the new health system model by promoting the idea of co-creation among different organizations and actors in the health and social context.

2.2 The organizational perspective of healthcare

The arguments made in the preceding paragraph highlight the marked distinctiveness of healthcare realities compared to other types of companies.

The subsequent organizational analysis is most useful in providing an indispensable knowledge base for strategic management choices.

The first element stimulating the organizational debate on healthcare companies is the distinct "brain-intensive" nature related to the high intensity of professional capital (Alvesson & Spicer, 2012; Hoff et al., 2016; Lega & Khan, 2021; Mills et al., 2015; Nonaka & Takeuchi 1995).

Drawing on Scott's (1965) view, it is possible to classify brain-intensive organizations into the two broad categories of autonomous professional organizations and heteronomous professional organizations. In the first case, control over professionals is exercised by the peer group: concrete example is given of professional firms. In the second case, control is more stringent and aimed at framing the professionals in a normative frame of reference also through the action of the administrative line, as is the case in healthcare organizations.

The genetic element common to both organizational solutions is professionalism. Understood as a form of organization of economic activities based on the self-organization of occupational communities, professionalism has been extensively explored in the sociological literature and crystallized, in particular, in the classical theories of Wilensky (1964) and Freidson (2001). The former identifies five typical steps in the establishment of a profession, which can be seen in the full-time commitment to a particular occupation, the establishment of specialized training schools, the emergence of professional associations, recognition by the state, and the development of a code of ethics.

Freison (2001), in turn, identifies certain critical elements necessary for the development and maintenance of a profession: a complex body of knowledge involving wide discretion in application, labor markets marked by peculiar rules of entry and operation, and an ideology rooted in higher values. Albeit with different perspectives, the two different sociological theories converge in identifying, at the basis of the professions, a highly specialized knowledge of exclusive competence of the group (Evetts, 2014). With respect to this expertise, there is a condition of thrusting information asymmetry under which neither the organization nor the patients can exercise control. Only professionals can govern decisions about their own production cycle (Irvine, 2004). This decision-making power, strongly anchored in the values of the scientific community to which they belong, overrides the very organization in which the professionals operate (Cruess & Cruess, 2020).

Professionalism is, therefore, the prerequisite for standardization of knowledge and mutual adjustment among professionals, which, in healthcare organizations, are the main mechanisms of coordination (Mintzberg, 1980).

The identifying elements of professionalism, common to the plethora of subcultures dialoguing within healthcare organizations, determine the wide divergence between what represent the two dominant cultures: the clinical culture proper to physicians and the managerial culture typical of administrators (Lindsay et al., 2020; Numerato et al., 2012).

The clinical culture drives the professional to act for the absolute good of the patient, under the guidance of his or her moral responsibility. This results in a natural and prevailing tension to the effectiveness of care rather than to compliance with the managerial rules typical of economic rationality.

The managerial and organizational perspective of healthcare 23

The managerial culture, on the other hand, interprets the concepts of effectiveness and quality of performance differently by paying attention, predominantly, to formal and procedural aspects, adherence to a rigid hierarchy of roles, centralization of power, and stringent control over organizational action.

The typical rules of managerial culture, as a result of the multiplication of regulatory production, have become more and more entrenched in the healthcare context, finding maximum expression in bureaucratic apparatuses (Harrison et al., 2015; Kruse et al., 2020). The latter, over time, have become indispensable to the functioning of the company. Such a scenario has seen the conflicts between the two opposing forces of professional autonomy, inspired by independence and freedom of action on the one hand and the organizational order based on standardized rules and procedures on the other, become even more acute.

The drives associated with increasing complexity, both organizational and environmental, have led heteronomous professional organizations to evolve toward the organizational model of professional bureaucracy theorized by Mintzberg (1980) and depicted in Figure 2.1. This model represents the ultimate expression of clinicians' domination of decision-making processes based on the mechanism of "pigeonholing," which tends to classify care needs into categories predetermined by the relevant scientific community with standardized programs and procedures (Glouberman & Mintzberg, 2001). Through this mechanism, professionals escape both peer and managerial control.

The purely clinical processes are complemented by support processes delivered by both health professionals and administrative staff. The clear predominance of clinical culture draws an organizational structure that certainly has peculiar dimensions and coordination mechanisms.

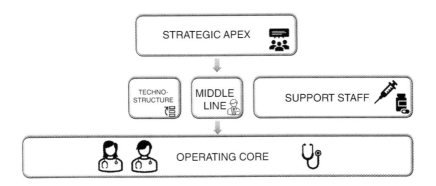

Figure 2.1 The professional bureaucracy.

Source: (authors' elaboration adapted from Mintzberg, 1980).

The strategic apex of the professional bureaucracy is traditionally represented by corporate management and is called upon to formulate strategy, provide oversight of organizational action, and manage relations with the external environment. In healthcare organizations, the strategic top management is responsible for adopting a corporate strategy that meets the needs of its catchment area while verifying the proper allocation of resources among the various components of the organization. In many cases, however, strategic direction is determined not by the exclusive action of top management but rather by the indirect pressure that professionals exert over time, through projects proposed and approved even after lengthy negotiations. In this regard, Mintzberg (2012, 2018) decisively debunks the myth of "management on top" by pointing out that in healthcare organizations, managerial exercise is employed through collaboration and the enhancement of skills distributed within the organization.

The middle line is represented by the operational line managers who serve as the link between the strategic top management and the operational base of the organization, called the operational core.

The technostructure consists of a set of professionals who are not directly engaged in the core processes of the organization but are charged with carrying out certain types of management-operational standardization and providing guidelines, objectives, and benchmarks. In healthcare, technostructure is effective only when, through its own techniques (of planning and control, organizational development, etc.), it succeeds in smoothing the processes of service production and delivery. The standardization of knowledge and skills tends, in fact, to reject all other mechanisms, including those designed by the technostructure, especially when aimed at influencing, directing, or planning the work of professionals.

Support staff includes the specific cross-line service functions such as safety, clinical engineering, information systems, and laboratory analysis. This part of the organization, although partly performed by health professionals, acts according to the typical mechanisms of mechanical bureaucracy related, essentially, to the standardization of work processes.

The operational core consists of the set of organizational actors who carry out the core activities of the organization related to the production or delivery of specialized services. In the healthcare context, the operational core is the most developed part and consists of the simple and complex operating units that deal with the delivery of healthcare services on the basis of complex, difficult-to-learn, but well-defined procedures. Professionals, who deal with unstructured problems, interact directly with their clients by receiving from them the information needed for specific service delivery.

The brain-intensive nature of the organization takes on an additional profile of complexity given by the cultural mosaic of professional and disciplinary groups that coexist there (Nancarrow & Borthwick, 2005). Each professional group is configured as a community that acts according to the typical rules of the clan. Within itself, each clan operates with a broad cohesion guaranteed by "clan control" or cloning-type control (Kohli & Kettinger, 2004), resulting from the set of values and expectations that guides the actions of the individual members. At the same time, intra-group solidarity generates friction and misunderstandings with other groups, especially at times of corporate resource allocation and power negotiation. The professional bureaucracy becomes, at times, a political arena—that is a battleground between professional groups aspiring for better organizational positions and spaces (Lega & De Pietro, 2005; Negri, 2021).

The scenario depicted from an organizational perspective highlights how any change within healthcare organizations must give due consideration to the relevant cultural and structural peculiarities by appropriately managing the possible "turf wars" or conflicts between professionals carrying different subcultures.

A winning strategy is one that activates win-win scenarios that place the supreme good of health at the center and, from the perspective of patient-centeredness, propose balanced solutions at both the clinical and management levels.

2.3 Process management in healthcare

The management and organizational challenge for healthcare is even more complex in light of the new health needs that characterize the current epidemiological scenario (e.g., Begun & Jiang, 2020; Haque, 2021; Lee & Lee, 2021; Tortorella et al., 2022). Acute infectious diseases are giving way to clinical problems related to the progressive aging of the population and to pathologies that are difficult to frame within a single disciplinary area.

In light, therefore, of the irrepressible need for a continuum of care among multiple specialist spheres (Gandhi et al., 2022; Hansen et al., 2019), a further effort of conceptual refinement and design in terms of polycentrism and recovery of the inter-organizational dimension is called for from the dominant paradigm of New Public Governance. The process vision, which leverages the integration of different medical specialties and professions and the powerful consolidation of inter-organizational and social-health relationships, represents in this context the response that best succeeds in interpreting new health needs. Socio-medical integration constitutes an indispensable lever of action that combines, in a balanced way, clinical treatment and patient-centeredness (Engberink et al., 2017) with a constant tension to the appropriate use of financial, human, and technological resources.

Organizational action, therefore, must shift the focus of attention from the vertical dimension, typical of organizational individualism, to the transversal dimension inherent in the process approach and capable of bridging the managerial and medical souls (FitzGerald & Ferlie, 2000; Marini, 2016).

Thus, if the process perspective aims at responding to new user care needs, from an organizational perspective it represents one of the greatest challenges to the traditional functional approach. It, in essence, shifts the focus from mere control over the process of value creation to the actual creation of value for the patient (Barnabè et al., 2019; McNulty & Ferlie, 2002) by accompanying it across the organization as well as on the terrain of inter-organizational relations.

Assuming the view of a process as a collection of activities that takes one or more kinds of input and creates an output that is of value to the customer (Hammer & Champy, 1993), organizational actors are urged to look at the goal of the organization as a whole—that is, the values that stand above the functional standards proper to individual organizational units. The organization is no longer understood as the sum of functional units or business units but as a set of interrelated, value-generating processes.

Healthcare processes, compared to those that can typically be recognized in other sectors, are characterized by their highly dynamic, complex, and increasingly multidisciplinary nature (Hesse-Biber, 2016).

Dynamism is related to changes brought about by technological developments or the discovery of new drugs. The continuous evolution of medical knowledge also results in the constant emergence of new therapeutic and diagnostic procedures that may invalidate current treatment pathways or require adaptations. The very discovery of new diseases, such as Covid-19, also requires healthcare organizations to implement new processes (Tortorella et al., 2022; Traylor et al., 2021; Wanat et al., 2021).

The complexity of healthcare processes is inherent in the very peculiarity of medical decisions, which involve large amounts of data to be exchanged and are complicated by the unpredictability of patients and treatments. Multidisciplinarity is related to the different knowledge involved in the patient journey and the resulting decision-making hubs that require an integrated view.

The classification of processes draws on the classic model developed by Porter (2001), which offers a detailed subdivision albeit one specifically addressed to industrial companies.

The model distinguishes two types of processes: primary or core processes, whose recipients are external to the company and which contribute directly to the generation of the output (product and service), and supporting processes, whose recipients are internal to the company and which do not intervene directly in the production of goods or delivery of services; the latter are equally indispensable, as they are functional to the primary ones (Kaplan & Porter, 2011).

The categories identified by Porter take on the following specificities within the healthcare context:

1   primary clinical-care processes: these represent the core processes consisting of the set of clinical activities carried out to solve a specific health problem. They have as their expected final output the resolution of the problem for which a patient came into contact with the healthcare facility;
2   supporting health processes: these consist of the set of activities that are clinical in nature, are strictly functional to the primary clinical-healthcare process, but do not produce a final health outcome; and
3   supportive administrative processes: these consist of the set of administrative activities that are useful for the proper conduct of the primary processes but do not involve direct patient involvement.

Focusing on the primary clinical-care (core) processes, the following episodes of care or phases can be recognized:

- the pre-admission (visit, appointment, etc.);
- the admission or "taking charge" of the patient by the referring company;
- diagnosis;
- preparation for treatment;
- treatment;
- rehabilitation;
- discharge;
- follow-up.

The construction of a comprehensive pathway by pathology involves the design of a continuum of care that allows for improving the quality of care, promoting safety, increasing patient satisfaction, and optimizing the use of resources (Lega & Sartirana, 2016). Adoption of such an organizational model allows for systematic comparison between the actual and optimal pathways, with the possibility of analyzing the reasons that generate outcomes and behaviors that differ from those expected.

Thus, processes represent the dimensions along which actions are developed so that a structure may also be efficient but, if the processes are not carried out properly, the results will not be satisfactory. If the monitoring of processes becomes the minimum goal to ensure sustainable levels of functionality and service, the improvement of processes that are structurally inefficient becomes the fundamental goal of any organization (Feibert et al., 2017). On the other hand, faulty healthcare processes have been found to be a major cause of professionals making technical errors that can severely compromise patient safety and even cost lives (Velo & Minuz, 2009).

The process described can be represented graphically as in Figure 2.2.

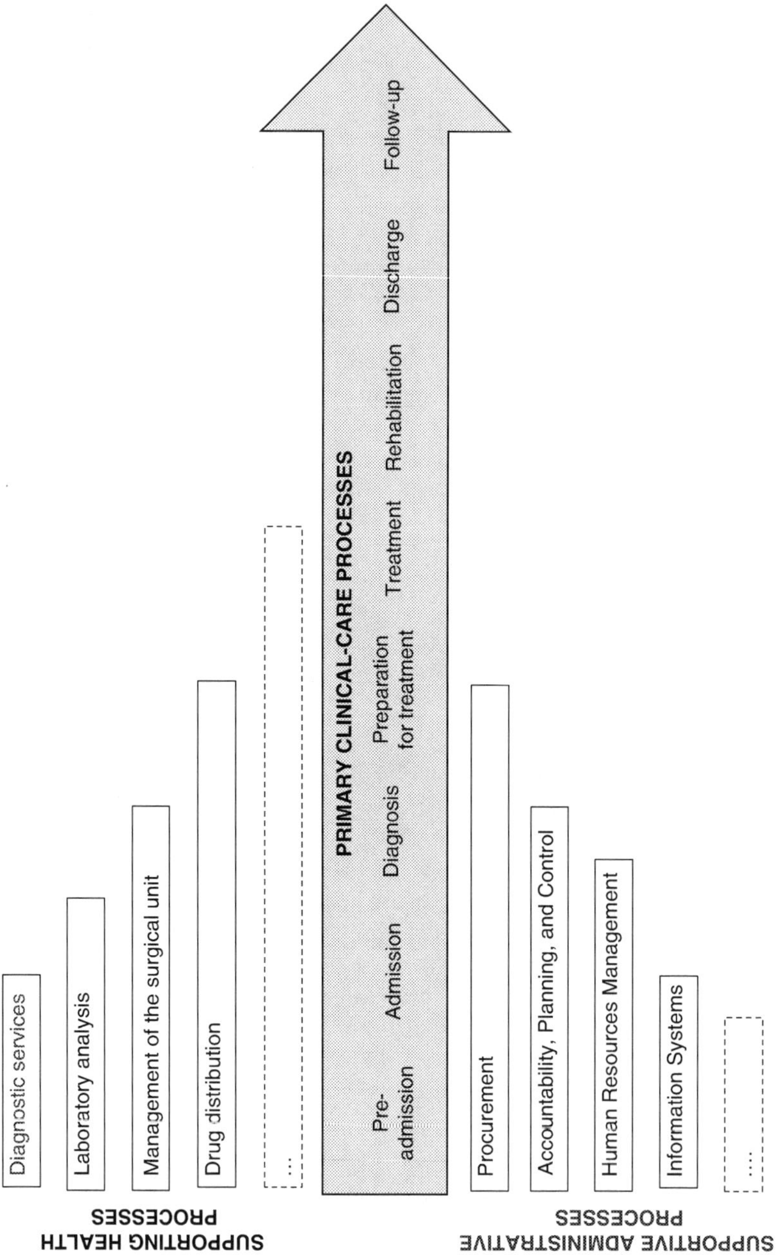

28 *Gabriella Piscopo*

Figure 2.2 The process approach within the healthcare context.
Source: (authors' elaboration).

2.4 The organizational approach of patient-centeredness

Like the organizational models outlined above, the adoption of a process approach also walks hand in hand with a new paradigm of health and renewed vision of medicine, which places the broader mission of "to care" alongside the mission of "to cure" (Aoun et al., 2018).

Concrete expressions of healthcare processes inspired by the logic of "to care" are integrated care pathways (Campbell et al., 1998). Such healthcare governance tools have arisen within different but in fact deeply interconnected disciplinary domains: Disease Management, Clinical Governance, and Process Management.

Although with different perspectives, each approach is oriented toward increasing the quality of care from a technical-specialist perspective by resolving the fragmentation of services and implementing periodic monitoring that is instrumental to continuous improvement (Sujan et al., 2021).

Disease Management stems from the reflections of clinical professionals who, for the purposes of expected health outcomes, understand the profound value of the interdependence that exists between different services and competencies. The focus is, therefore, shifted away from access to the individual service and to the continuum of care—that is, the coordination of the resources needed by the citizen on the path he or she takes to the entire healthcare system. Disease Management produces an initial reorganization of care with specific health conditions and in specialized settings (Harris Jr., 1996).

The second strand of Clinical Governance thinking arose, at the institutional level, in 1998 within the framework of the UK Health Plan "A First Class Service" and, at the theoretical level, from Scally and Donaldson's (1998) definition like a system through which NHS organizations are accountable for continuously improving the quality of their services and safeguarding high standards of care by creating an environment in which excellence in clinical care will flourish.

Clinical Governance (CG), based on a newfound dialog between institutions and scientific societies, proposes high clinical care quality standards for the entire healthcare system along with clinical audit and risk management mechanisms aimed at verifying quality levels translated into practice. Clinical Governance lays the foundation for the spread of Evidence-Based Medicine as well as the increasing focus on cost containment (Braithwaite & Travaglia, 2008). In addition, the accountability of clinical knowledge and the continuous learning it promotes pushes to overcome the propensity for an often "personalistic" clinical practice inspired by the professional beliefs of individual actors. The very practice of defensive medicine, aimed at overprescribing examinations rather than identifying only those activities deemed appropriate, tends to be broken down.

The third strand of Process Management, which has a distinctly managerial matrix, in fact systematizes the underlying principles of both Disease Management and Clinical Governance (Degeling et al., 2004). For each health condition, it interprets diagnostic and treatment pathways as a unified delivery process guided by the patient's needs and governed by standards of evidence and good clinical care practice. The focus is shifted to the health production process, understood as a concatenation of intakes between different professionals and different care settings that manage the complex care process with respect to the health problem. The "final product" is not given simply by the delivery of healthcare but by the recovery, maintenance, and improvement of the level of health.

The increasing interaction between the three process types and the increasingly multidisciplinary nature of the processes requires a collaborative effort of professionals with different skills, knowledge, and organizational culture. Each professional, within the different care settings and organizational units, is responsible for the results of appropriateness, integration, expenditure, and efficiency profile. The same conditions of effectiveness are no longer defined individually and in isolation by the individual professional but, rather, through the expanded comparison of those who treat the same type of patients, albeit with different specialized approaches.

The process view, therefore, constitutes a useful managerial tool that enables the organization to integrate the different drives of professional autonomy that, traditionally, tend to hinder protocol sharing and teamwork (Weller et al., 2014).

If the healthcare process represents the natural management object of the process-based view (Vera & Kuntz, 2007), the care pathway constitutes its governing tool through which the patient receives care as well as the sequence of actions that must be carried out by the different professionals involved in the management of the health problem.

The patient pathway, in a logic of continuous quality improvement, designs the best possible temporal and spatial sequence on the basis of the technical-scientific knowledge and the professional and technological resources available (Yang et al., 2012).

Taking value production as a guiding criterion, on the one hand it is possible to recognize the critical activities that make the process slow and complicated, and on the other hand it is possible to identify those actions that generate improved results from the point of view of the patient's health but also on the economic, managerial, and organizational level. Therefore, pathways make it possible to touch the three fundamental actors in the care process: the patient-user, since pathways represent an important tool for his or her active involvement; the organization, since pathways make it possible to identify the actors involved by establishing the roles and responsibilities of each in the care process; and, finally, the caregivers involved, since pathways are capable of influencing clinical practice through confrontation and learning and are useful in reducing the unjustified variability of their behaviors.

The patient pathway finds its operational expression in clinical pathways, developed in the United States starting in the 1980s and then spread with different time steps in Canada with Care Maps, in Anglo-Saxon culture with Integrated Care Pathways, and in Italy with PDTAs (Percorsi Diagnostico-Terapeutici Assistenziali).

This managerial tool, an expression of the new "patient-centered" health paradigm (Askeer et al., 2021), designs the overall pathway that a patient must take within one or more health facilities, defining the relationship between activities and clinical-assistance practices useful for meeting screening, diagnostic, treatment, and follow-up needs related to a specific health need. Starting with the clear definition of goals of care based on evidence, best practice, and patient expectations, they facilitate communication between professionals as well as among professionals, patients, and family members by identifying appropriate resources for each step.

From an organizational perspective, the spread of clinical pathways is a significant moment for the dimension of work and, in particular, for collaborative practice defined by the World Health Organization (WHO) as the result of multiple health workers from different professional backgrounds providing comprehensive services by working with patients, families and communities to deliver high-quality patient care.

This collaborative approach to work results in overcoming the old artifacts focused on the effectiveness of individual tasks. Indeed, the multidimensional aspect of care processes enhances the interaction between different professionals, collaboration, and the propensity for innovation and learning (see Di Vincenzo & Iacopino, 2022). Traditional work routines are eliminated in favor of high-involvement work that can generate innovation, growth, and learning (Al-Agry, 2021; Kilroy et al., 2017).

The joint action of different health professionals is expressed in the different forms of multidisciplinarity, trans-disciplinarity, and interprofessional collaboration.

Multidisciplinarity sees different professionals collaborating on a common project while retaining their autonomy of scientific domain, whereas trans-disciplinarity activates an exchange of skills, knowledge and experience that transcends the boundaries of traditional disciplines. Interprofessional Collaboration (IPC) sees different professional groups, physicians, and clinical staff engaged to act as consultants in support of specific care needs unique to a well-defined group of patients. This working approach is identified by the WHO as the ideal solution that allows the team to express the maximum potential of care by enhancing the synergy between them. In fact, the collaborative approach arises from the design phase of the patient pathway and involves multispecialized and multiprofessional teams pertaining to both the clinical and managerial spheres. Moreover, the opportunity to be at the same work table constitutes an important opportunity not only to reflect on the clinical and administrative activities of the organization in which one works but also to lay the foundations of a high-trust interprofessional context. Doctors, nurses, and other health professionals, working together, strengthen awareness about each other's competencies, opening up the process of decision-making to a collective dimension supported by a constructive exchange of knowledge, skills, and ideas.

2.5 Healthcare process redesign and the challenge for the birth path

The effectiveness of organizational action inspired by the process view is closely linked to the constant striving for improvement in terms of appropriateness of care and effectiveness and efficiency of management (Ferreira et al., 2020). Thus, the process-based organizational model implies the mastery and application of redesign approaches and tools.

Redesign represents a management approach aimed at improving process efficiency by modifying or eliminating activities that do not add value for the customer. It involves processes of mapping, deconstruction, and reconstruction in order to define a more efficient and customer-focused process.

Retraining the process and structure of the organization means prioritizing needs and outcomes, improving the "customer experience" in terms of perceived quality, and reducing time and costs in an environment of limited healthcare resources in the face of inexorably increasing demand.

Within the healthcare context, Business Process Reengineering (BPR) (Bertolini et al., 2011) and Business Process Improvement (BPI) (Ahmed et al., 2019; Aloini et al., 2022) represent the approaches to redesign that have been most popular in an attempt to compose the fragmentation of different specialized units and improve service quality. The thriving literature on BPR builds on the classic assumptions formulated by Hammer and Champy (1993), who define the process of reengineering as the fundamental rethinking and radical redesign of business processes aimed at achieving extraordinary improvements in critical performance parameters such as cost, quality, service and speed. According to the authors, information and communication technologies alone are not sufficient to achieve improvements in business performance; rather, investment in ICT (Information and Communication Technology) must be followed by a process of radical reform of the organizational structure and the way the enterprise operates (Haluza & Jungwirth, 2015). The rethinking of the enterprise proposed by the authors aims to design a modern, proactive organization that is able to think jointly about strategy and processes, products, and services, using creativity, knowledge, information, and information technology.

A second approach in the literature, the gradualist approach called BPI, starts from criticisms of the radical approach. Specifically, according to Davenport (1993), a radical approach is not always necessary, since increasing the level of performance can also be achieved through progressive business process improvement. Davenport, focusing on the use of technology as an "enabling factor," proposes a more structured and controlled approach that alternates moments of radical reengineering with phases of continuous control and improvement.

Considering these two antithetical visions, empirical studies have shown (e.g., Netjes et al., 2009) that BPR is better suited to the healthcare context because of its power to redefine the organizational model, to intervene in terms of cost containment, and to affect the improved fluidity of cure and care processes.

Moreover, within BPR-inspired organizational practice, two approaches have since developed that are further diversified from each other: the pure radical approach and the "radical-contingent" approach. The former is representative of the "clean-slate rhetoric", which argues for the effectiveness of a deep intervention that disregards the previous pattern of the organization within a kind of "institutional amnesia" (Grint & Case, 2000). The latter, on the other hand, is inspired by a contingent perspective and imposes any intervention, however radical, on the basis of a preliminary analysis of the organization's status quo.

Between the two divergent visions, in this text's own attempt to identify possible BPR trajectories for the birth path, Lega and Khan's (2021) propose the idea of not neglecting such a highly professional heritage of expertise stratified over time. In fact, the value of the latter can never be replaced by the organizational precision of a made-to-order design.

Generally, the reengineering process consists of the following steps:

1. process selection;
2. the understanding of the process, useful for content, performance, and criticality analysis;
3. the implementation of the actual reengineering.

The first phase involves the mapping of the current process, the so-called "as is," within which any inefficiencies, such as bottlenecks, high lead times (the time it takes to go through each process step), or, again, duplication of operations, can be identified. Starting from the critical elements that hinder the achievement of expected performance, envisaged in the second phase, the new process called "to be" is modeled.

The optimal representation of the process is a useful tool both for the healthcare company, as it is an incentive to improve service standards, and for the patient, as he or she will have all the information about the expected treatment at his or her disposal. This circumstance will help to reduce the patient's anxiety related to the need for healthcare through greater trust in the organization and greater empowerment in the treatment process.

The process view represents a tool that is as useful as ever in the analysis of the childbirth event and strictly functional to the challenge it poses in terms of redesign.

The birth path, as highlighted in Chapter 1, through its multidimensional nature is a significant expression of the complexity that a health service can present as well as the transversality that the same can take on the social-health front. Conducting the organizational analysis of the birth path means recognizing and enhancing the bio-psycho-social model of health that considers childbirth as a biological, social, and affective event.

The first step, necessary for the purposes of the analysis, is to define the boundaries within which the birth-related experience takes shape. Reported boundaries are rather fluid since there is no univocal model, but it depends on the cultural assumptions of each country, health policies, and the role attributed to the different professionals involved in the journey.

Typically, the boundaries are strictly adjacent to the birth point when the medical model—which conceives of childbirth as a possible source of risk and, as such, to be managed exclusively within the hospital—is prevalent.

While this model has positively impacted maternal/infant morbidity and mortality rates at the international level, over time it has favored an approach that is sometimes over-medicalized, with the risk of inappropriate care interventions with respect to the natural evolution of the pathway.

The second model is the Midwifery Model, which promotes and values the physiological nature of birth by placing the woman at the center of care while clearly not excluding medical intervention when necessary (Berg et al., 2012). The latter has gained wide international recognition, especially following recognition by the development of the Midwifery2030 Pathway (ten Hoope-Bender et al., 2016), a new framework for the provision of woman-centered sexual, reproductive, maternal, newborn, and adolescent healthcare contained in The State of the World's Midwifery 2014. Specifically, the group of experts in the field of midwifery who internationally worked on the framework identified four stages in a woman's reproductive life: (1) pre-pregnancy, (2) pregnancy, (3) labor and birth, and (4) postnatal.

In the wake of this classification and the midwifery model, it is possible to understand the birth path from the time when a woman decides that she wants to become pregnant and adopts all behaviors aimed at doing so, to the first life cycle of the child, which is conventionally identified as the first 1,000 days of life. The analysis of the birth path will, therefore, move within said boundaries of action in order to represent the complete mapping of the relationships between patient, professionals, and organizations in order to propose, in the last chapter, a possible redesign of the value constellation.

References

Abraham, M., & Moretz, J. G. (2012). Implementing patient-and family-centered care: part I-understanding the challenges. *Pediatric Nursing*, *38*(1), 44.

Adinolfi, P. (2004). *Il mito dell'azienda. L'innovazione gestionale e organizzativa nelle amministrazioni pubbliche*. McGraw Hill Companies.

Adinolfi, P., & Borgonovi, E. (2018). *The myths of health care*. Switzerland: Springer International Publishing AG.

Ahmed, E. S., Ahmad, M. N., & Othman, S. H. (2019). Business process improvement methods in healthcare: a comparative study. *International Journal of Health Care Quality*

Assurance, Jun 10; *32*(5), 887–908. doi: 10.1108/IJHCQA-07-2017-0116. PMID: 31195926

Al-Agry, D. F. (2021). High-involvement human resource practices and their impact on organizational ambidexterity: the mediating role of employees' ambidextrous behaviors. *Global Business and Organizational Excellence*, *40*(5), 23–36.

Aloini, D., Benevento, E., Stefanini, A., & Zerbino, P. (2022). Transforming healthcare ecosystems through blockchain: opportunities and capabilities for business process innovation. *Technovation*, *118*(2022), 102557, ISSN 0166-4972.

Alvesson, M., & Spicer, A. (2012). Critical leadership studies: the case for critical performativity. *Human relations*, *65*(3), 367–390.

Andrews, R., Beynon, M. J., & McDermott, A. (2019). Configurations of new public management reforms and the efficiency, effectiveness and equity of public healthcare systems: a fuzzy-set qualitative comparative analysis. *Public Management Review*, *21*(8), 1236–1260.

Anttonen, A., Häikiö, L., Stefánsson, K., & Sipilä, J. (2012). Universalism and the challenge of diversity. *Welfare State, Universalism and Diversity* (pp. 1–15). Cheltenham: Edward Elgar.

Aoun, S. M., Hogden, A., & Kho, L. K. (2018). "Until there is a cure, there is care": a person-centered approach to supporting the wellbeing of people with Motor Neurone Disease and their family carers. *European Journal for Person Centered Healthcare*, *6*(2), 320–328.

Akseer, R., Connolly, M., Cosby, J., Frost, G., Kanagarajah, R. R., & Lim, S. H. E. (2021). Clinician–patient relationships after two decades of a paradigm of patient-centered care. *International Journal of Healthcare Management*, *14*(3), 888–897.

Babiker, A., El Husseini, M., Al Nemri, A., Al Frayh, A., Al Juryyan, N., Faki, M. O., ... & Al Zamil, F. (2014). Health care professional development: working as a team to improve patient care. *Sudanese Journal of Paediatrics*, *14*(2), 9.

Barnabè, F., Guercini, J., & Perna, M. D. (2019). Assessing performance and value-creation capabilities in lean healthcare: insights from a case study. *Public Money & Management*, *39*(7), 503–511.

Barzelay, M. (2001). The new public management. In *The New Public Management*. University of California Press.

Begun, J. W., & Jiang, H. J. (2020). Health care management during COVID-19: insights from complexity science. *NEJM Catalyst Innovations in Care Delivery*, October 9, *1*(5), 1–12.

Berg, M., Ólafsdóttir, Ó. A., & Lundgren, I. (2012). A midwifery model of woman-centred childbirth care–In Swedish and Icelandic settings. *Sexual & Reproductive Healthcare*, *3*(2), 79–87.

Bertolini, M., Bevilacqua, M., Ciarapica, F. E., & Giacchetta, G. (2011). Business process re-engineering in healthcare management: a case study. *Business Process Management Journal*, *17*, 42–66.

Bradby, H., Humphris, R., & Padilla, B. (2020). Universalism, diversity and norms: gratitude, healthcare and welfare chauvinism. *Critical Public Health*, *30*(2), 166–178.

Braithwaite, J., & Travaglia, J. F. (2008). An overview of clinical governance policies, practices and initiatives. *Australian Health Review*, *32*(1), 10–22.

Byrkjeflot, H. (2005). The rise of a healthcare state?. *Recent Healthcare Reforms in Norway*. Working Paper 15 - 2005, 1–38.

Campbell, H., Hotchkiss, R., Bradshaw, N., & Porteous, M. (1998). Integrated care pathways. *BMJ, 316*(7125), 133–137.

Carlini, J., Bahudin, D., Michaleff, Z. A., Plunkett, E., Shé, É. N., Clark, J., & Cardona, M. (2022). Discordance and concordance on perception of quality care at end of life between older patients, caregivers and clinicians: a scoping review. *European Geriatric Medicine*, Feb; *13*(1), 87–99. doi: 10.1007/s41999-021-00549-6. Epub 2021 Aug 12. PMID: 34386928; PMCID: PMC8359918.

Churruca, K., Pomare, C., Ellis, L. A., Long, J. C., & Braithwaite, J. (2019). The influence of complexity: a bibliometric analysis of complexity science in healthcare. *BMJ open, 9*(3), e027308.

Costa Oliveira, H., Lima Rodrigues, L., & Craig, R. (2021). Reasons for bureaucracy in the management of Portuguese public enterprise hospitals–an institutional logics perspective. *International Journal of Public Administration, 44*, 1–10.

Cruess, R. L., & Cruess, S. R. (2020). Professionalism, communities of practice, and medicine's social contract. *The Journal of the American Board of Family Medicine, 33*(Supplement), S50–S56.

Davenport, T. H. (1993). *Process innovation: reengineering work through information technology*. Harvard Business Press.

Degeling, P. J., Maxwell, S., Iedema, R., & Hunter, D. J. (2004). Making clinical governance work. *BMJ, 329*(7467), 679–681.

Di Vincenzo, F., & Iacopino, V. (2022). 'Catching the new': exploring the impact of professional networks on innovative work behavior in healthcare. *Creativity and Innovation Management, 31*(1), 141–151.

Dickinson, H. (2016). From new public management to new public governance: the implications for a 'new public service'. *The Three Sector Solution: Delivering public policy in collaboration with not-for-profits and business, 41*, 41–60.

Engberink, A. O., Badin, M., Serayet, P., Pavageau, S., Lucas, F., Bourrel, G., ... & Senesse, P. (2017). Patient-centeredness to anticipate and organize an end-of-life project for patients receiving at-home palliative care: a phenomenological study. *BMC Family Practice, 18*(1), 1–8.

Evetts, J. (2014). The concept of professionalism: professional work, professional practice and learning. In *International handbook of research in Professional and Practice-based Learning* (pp. 29–56). Dordrecht: Springer.

Feibert, D. C., Jacobsen, P., & Wallin, M. (2017). Improving healthcare logistics processes. *DTU Management Engineering, Denmark*. PhD thesis. 1–375.

Ferreira, D. C., Nunes, A. M., & Marques, R. C. (2020). Operational efficiency vs clinical safety, care appropriateness, timeliness, and access to health care. *Journal of Productivity Analysis, 53*(3), 355–375.

FitzGerald, L, & Ferlie, E. (2000). Professionals: back to the future?. *Human Relations, 53*(5), 713–739.

Freidson, E. (2001). *Professionalism, the third logic: On the practice of knowledge*. University of Chicago press.

Gandhi, S., Gandhi, S., Dash, U., & Suresh Babu, M. (2022). Predictors of the utilisation of continuum of maternal health care services in India. *BMC Health Services Research, 22*(1), 1–12.

Geampana, A., & Perrotta, M. (2022). Accounting for complexity in healthcare innovation debates: Professional views on the use of new IVF treatments. *Health: An Interdisciplinary Journal*, https://doi.org/10.1177/13634593221074874.

Glouberman, S., & Mintzberg, H. (2001). Managing the care of health and the cure of disease—Part II: Integration. *Health Care Management Review*, Winter; 26(1), 70–84.

Gow, J.I., & Dufour, C. (2000). Is the new public management a paradigm? Does it matter? *International Review of Administrative Sciences*, 66, 573–597.

Grint, K. & Case, P. (2000). 'Now Where Were We? BPR Lotus-Eaters and Corporate Amnesia'. In Knights, D. & Willmott, H. (eds), *The reengineering revolution: critical studies of corporate change* (pp. 26–49). London: Sage.

Hall, D., Grimaldi, E., Gunter, H. M., Møller, J., Serpieri, R., & Skedsmo, G. (2015). Educational reform and modernisation in Europe: the role of national contexts in mediating the new public management. *European Educational Research Journal*, 14(6), 487–507.

Haluza, D., & Jungwirth, D. (2015). ICT and the future of health care: aspects of health promotion. *International Journal of Medical Informatics*, 84(1), 48–57.

Hammer, M., & Champy, J. (1993). Business process reengineering. *London: Nicholas Brealey*, 444(10), 730–755.

Haque, A. (2021). The COVID-19 pandemic and the role of responsible leadership in health care: thinking beyond employee well-being and organisational sustainability. *Leadership in Health Services*. (Bradf Engl). Feb 8; 34(1). 52–68. doi: 10.1108/LHS-09-2020-0071. PMID: 33818971.

Hansen, M. P., Saunders, M. M., Kollauf, C. R., & Santiago-Rotchford, L. (2019). Clinical nurse specialists: leaders in managing patients with chronic conditions. *Nursing Economics*, 37(2), 103–109.

Harris Jr, J. M. (1996). Disease management: new wine in new bottles?. *Annals of Internal Medicine*, 124(9), 838–842.

Harrison, M., Milbers, K., Hudson, M., & Bansback, N. (2017). Do patients and health care providers have discordant preferences about which aspects of treatments matter most? Evidence from a systematic review of discrete choice experiments. *BMJ open*, 7(5), e014719.

Harrison, S., Hupe, P., & Hill, M. (2015). Street-level bureaucracy and professionalism in health services. In Hupe, P., Hill M., Buffat A. *Understanding Street-level Bureaucracy*, Bristol University Press, 61–78.

Hesse-Biber, S. (2016). Doing interdisciplinary mixed methods health care research: working the boundaries, tensions, and synergistic potential of team-based research. *Qualitative Health Research*, 26(5), 649–658.

Hoff, T., Sutcliffe, K. M., & Young, G. J. (Eds.). (2016). *The healthcare professional workforce: understanding human capital in a changing industry*. Oxford University Press.

Irvine, D. H. (2004). Time for hard decisions on patient-centred professionalism. *Medical Journal of Australia*, 181(5), 271–274.

Joshi, M., Ransom, E. R., Nash, D. B., & Ransom, S. B. (Eds.). (2014). *The healthcare quality book: vision, strategy, and tools*. Chicago, IL, USA: Health Administration Press.

Jun, J. S. (2007). *The social construction of public administration: interpretive and critical perspectives*. SUNY Press.

Kannampallil, T. G., Schauer, G. F., Cohen, T., & Patel, V. L. (2011). Considering complexity in healthcare systems. *Journal of Biomedical Informatics*, 44(6), 943–947.

Kaplan, R. S., & Porter, M. E. (2011). How to solve the cost crisis in health care. *Harvard Business Review*, 89(9), 46–52.

Kilroy, S., Flood, P. C., Bosak, J., & Chênevert, D. (2017). Perceptions of high-involvement work practices, person-organization fit, and burnout: a time-lagged study of health care employees. *Human Resource Management, 56*(5), 821–835.

Koelewijn, W. T., Ehrenhard, M. L., Groen, A. J., & Van Harten, W. H. (2012). Intra-organizational dynamics as drivers of entrepreneurship among physicians and managers in hospitals of western countries. *Social Science & Medicine, 75*(5), 795–800.

Kohli, R., & Kettinger, W. J. (2004). Informating the clan: Controlling physicians' costs and outcomes. *MIS Quarterly*, Sep., 2004, *28*(3), 363–394.

Kruse, F. M., Ligtenberg, W. M., Oerlemans, A. J., Groenewoud, S., & Jeurissen, P. (2020). How the logics of the market, bureaucracy, professionalism and care are reconciled in practice: an empirical ethics approach. *BMC Health Services Research, 20*(1), 1–16.

Kunz, R., & Oxman, A. D. (1998). The unpredictability paradox: review of empirical comparisons of randomised and non-randomised clinical trials. *BMJ, 317*(7167), 1185–1190.

Lega, F. (2005). *Organizational design and development for health care services*. McGraw-Hill.

Lega, F., & De Pietro, C. (2005). Converging patterns in hospital organization: beyond the professional bureaucracy. *Health Policy, 74*(3), 261–281.

Lega, F., & Khan, U. (2021). Health leadership in transition. In *Health Management 2.0*. Emerald Publishing Limited.

Lega, F., & Sartirana, M. (2016). Making doctors manage … but how? Recent developments in the Italian NHS. *BMC Health Services Research, 16*(2), 65–72.

Lee, S. M., & Lee, D. (2021). Opportunities and challenges for contactless healthcare services in the post-COVID-19 Era. *Technological Forecasting and Social Change, 167*, 120712.

Leicht, K. T., Walter, T., Sainsaulieu, I., & Davies, S. (2009). New public management and new professionalism across nations and contexts. *Current Sociology, 57*(4), 581–605.

Lindsay, C. F., Kumar, M., & Juleff, L. (2020). Operationalising lean in healthcare: the impact of professionalism. *Production Planning & Control, 31*(8), 629–643.

Lukas, C. V., Holmes, S. K., Cohen, A. B., Restuccia, J., Cramer, I. E., Shwartz, M., & Charns, M. P. (2007). Transformational change in health care systems: an organizational model. *Health Care Management Review, 32*(4), 309–320.

Marini, M. G. (2016). Designing health care based on patient's needs and rights. In *Narrative Medicine* (pp. 81–91). Cham: Springer.

Monrouxe, L. V., & Rees, C. E. (2017). *Healthcare professionalism: improving practice through reflections on workplace dilemmas*. John Wiley & Sons.

Miller, B. F., & Hubley, S. H. (2017). The history of fragmentation and the promise of integration. *Handbook of Psychological Assessment in Primary Care Settings, 55*–73.

Mills, G. R., Phiri, M., Erskine, J., & Price, A. D. (2015). Rethinking healthcare building design quality: an evidence-based strategy. *Building Research & Information, 43*(4), 499–515.

Mintzberg, H. (1980). Structure in 5's: a synthesis of the research on organization design. *Management Science, 26*(3), 322–341.

Mintzberg, H. (2012). Managing the myths of health care. *World Hospitals and Health Services, 48*(3), 4–7.

Mintzberg, H. (2018). Managing the myths of health care. In *The Myths of Health Care* (pp. 3–11). Cham: Springer.

McNulty, T., & Ferlie, E. (2002). *Reengineering health care: the complexities of organizational transformation*. Oxford University Press.

Nancarrow, S. A., & Borthwick, A. M. (2005). Dynamic professional boundaries in the healthcare workforce. *Sociology of Health & Illness, 27*(7), 897–919.

Negri, J. J. (2021). Bureaucracy and politics. In *The emerald handbook of public administration in Latin America*. Emerald Publishing Limited.

Netjes, M., Mans, R. S., Reijers, H. A., van der Aalst, W. M., & Vanwersch, R. J. (2009). BPR best practices for the healthcare domain. In *International conference on business process management* (pp. 605–616). Berlin, Heidelberg: Springer.

Nguyen, T. L. H., & Nagase, K. (2021). Patient satisfaction and loyalty to the healthcare organization. *International Journal of Pharmaceutical and Healthcare Marketing, 15*(4), 496–515. https://doi.org/10.1108/IJPHM-02-2020-0011

Noblet, A. J., & Rodwell, J. J. (2009). Identifying the predictors of employee health and satisfaction in an NPM environment: testing a comprehensive and non-linear demand-control-support model. *Public Management Review, 11*(5), 663–683.

Nonaka, I. T., & Takeuchi, H. (1995). *The knowledge creating company*.

Numerato, D., Salvatore, D., & Fattore, G. (2012). The impact of management on medical professionalism: a review. *Sociology of Health & Illness, 34*(4), 626–644.

O'Flynn, J. (2007). From new public management to public value: paradigmatic change and managerial implications. *Australian Journal of Public Administration, 66*(3), 353–366.

Osborne, S. P. (2006). *The new public governance?*. Taylor & Francis.

Pimentel, M. P. T., Choi, S., Fiumara, K., Kachalia, A., & Urman, R. D. (2021). Safety culture in the operating room: variability among perioperative healthcare workers. *Journal of Patient Safety, 17*(6), 412–416.

Porter, M. E. (2001). The value chain and competitive advantage. *Understanding Business Processes, 2*, 50–66.

Rouse, W. B., & Serban, N. (2014). *Understanding and Managing the Complexity of Healthcare*. MIT Press.

Scally, G., & Donaldson, L. J. (1998). Clinical governance and the drive for quality improvement in the new NHS in England. *BMJ, 317*(7150), 61–65.

Scott, W. R. (1965). Field methods in the study of organizations. *Handbook of Organizations*, 261–304.

Sculpher, M. J., Pang, F. S., Manca, A., Drummond, M. F., Golder, S., Urdahl, H., ... & Eastwood, A. (2004). Generalisability in economic evaluation studies in healthcare: a review and case studies. *Health Technology Assessment (Winchester, England), 8*(49), iii–iv.

Simonet, D. (2015). The new public management theory in the British health care system: a critical review. *Administration & Society, 47*(7), 802–826.

Spena, T. R., & Cristina, M. (2019). Practising innovation in the healthcare ecosystem: the agency of third-party actors. *Journal of Business & Industrial Marketing*.

Sujan, M., Pickup, L., Bowie, P., Hignett, S., Ives, F., Vosper, H., & Rashid, N. (2021). The contribution of human factors and ergonomics to the design and delivery of safe future healthcare. *Future Healthcare Journal, 8*(3), e574.

Tenbensel, T., Silwal, P., & Walton, L. (2021). Overwriting new public management with new public governance in new zealand's approach to health system improvement. *Journal of Health Organization and Management, 35*(8), 1046–1061(16).

ten Hoope-Bender, P., Lopes, S. T. C., Nove, A., Michel-Schuldt, M., Moyo, N. T., Bokosi, M., ... & Homer, C. (2016). Midwifery 2030: a woman's pathway to health. What does this mean?. *Midwifery, 32*, 1–6.

Tortorella, G. L., Fogliatto, F. S., Saurin, T. A., Tonetto, L. M., & McFarlane, D. (2022). Contributions of Healthcare 4.0 digital applications to the resilience of healthcare organizations during the COVID-19 outbreak. *Technovation*, *111*, 102379.

Traylor, A. M., Tannenbaum, S. I., Thomas, E. J., & Salas, E. (2021). Helping healthcare teams save lives during COVID-19: insights and countermeasures from team science. *American Psychologist*, *76*(1), 1.

Velo, G. P., & Minuz, P. (2009). Medication errors: prescribing faults and prescription errors. *British Journal of Clinical Pharmacology*, *67*(6), 624–628.

Vera, A., & Kuntz, L. (2007). Process-based organization design and hospital efficiency. *Health Care Management Review*, *32*(1), 55–65.

Wanat, M., Hoste, M., Gobat, N., Anastasaki, M., Böhmer, F., Chlabicz, S., ... & Tonkin-Crine, S. (2021). Transformation of primary care during the COVID-19 pandemic: experiences of healthcare professionals in eight European countries. *British Journal of General Practice*, *71*(709), e634–e642.

Weller, J., Boyd, M., & Cumin, D. (2014). Teams, tribes and patient safety: overcoming barriers to effective teamwork in healthcare. *Postgraduate Medical Journal*, *90*(1061), 149–154.

Wilensky, H. L. (1964). The professionalization of everyone?. *American Journal of Sociology*, *70*(2), 137–158.

Yang, H., Li, W., Liu, K., & Zhang, J. (2012). Knowledge-based clinical pathway for medical quality improvement. *Information Systems Frontiers*, *14*(1), 105–117.

3 The birth path as a process: criticalities and cesarean section

Gabriella Piscopo and Margherita Ruberto

3.1 The stages of the birth path

The process underlying the birth path is analyzed by means of the flow-charting technique, which makes it possible to graphically represent the sequence of activities involving the woman during the different phases described below.

In order to reflect on possible levels of generalization in the international context, this study omits the consideration of support processes and focuses in details only on the following core processes: (1) preconception care, (2) access to the birth path with pregnancy status assessment and first visit – and, consequently, access to the low-risk (physiological) pregnancy pathway and medium/high-risk pregnancy pathway, (3) labor and delivery phase, and (4) puerperium phase (Figure 3.1).

The analysis conducted is the result of a multidisciplinary reading that tends to capture the complex nature of the childbirth event. In particular, the organizational perspective provides the conceptual and methodological framework that frames the phenomenon as a process that unfolds on an inter-organizational terrain. The clinical perspective, in turn, expresses the disciplinary mastery related to the birth path, validating the multi-perspective view that the book proposes.

3.2 Preconception care

The preconception phase (see Ragusa et al., 2021) can be identified in its genesis with the woman's or couple's request for access to the consultatory. The gynecologist and/or the midwife are the professionals assigned to initiate the pathway and manage the first interview. The strategic cognitive tool for this phase is the personal and family history (Löwy, 2017). If carried out accurately, it is essential in order to put in place behaviors that are protective of the good health of the couple and the potential child.

If risk factors are identified during these assessments, the couple and/or woman are referred to specialized services. In making recommendations,

42 *Gabriella Piscopo and Margherita Ruberto*

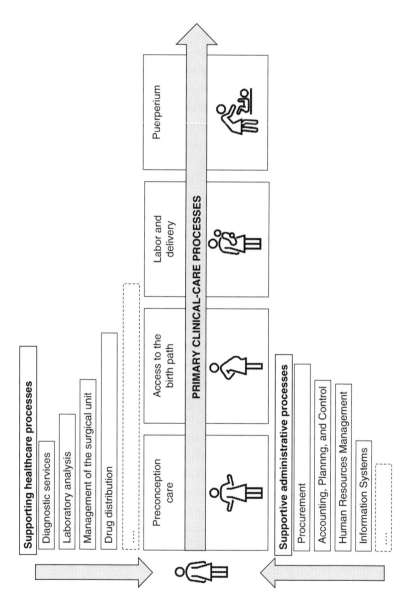

Figure 3.1 The Value Systems in the birth path.
Source: (authors' elaboration).

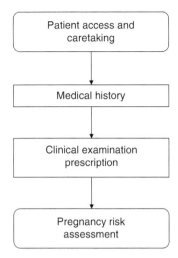

Figure 3.2 Preconception phase.
Source: (authors' elaboration).

health professionals estimate the potential for pregnancy-related morbidity and mortality to assess whether the patient is at high, moderate, or low risk.

Patients with serious medical conditions are at extremely high risk of maternal mortality or severe morbidity (Geller et al., 2018; Kozhimannil et al., 2020; Narayan & Nelson-Piercy, 2017). In such circumstances, pregnancy should be undertaken only after fully weighing these extreme risks. Patients with moderate risk have higher probability of adverse maternal, fetal, or neonatal outcomes. Such patients include women with medical complications, such as hypertension or diabetes, so a visit to a general practitioner or specialist prior to pregnancy is necessary. Patients with a history of previous pregnancy complications (see Grandi et al., 2019), such as preterm delivery or preeclampsia, should be referred to a midwife or maternal-fetal medicine specialist for preconception counseling (Figure 3.2).

This stage is very important, because it reduces the risks of malformations that can occur in the very early stages of embryo development. If adverse reproductive outcomes are highlighted in time, in fact, it is possible to adopt protective behaviors such as supplementing folic acid, maintaining a healthy lifestyle, and obtaining immunization against certain diseases that, if contracted during pregnancy, can harm the fetus.

3.3 Access to the birth path

Once pregnancy status has been established, the woman can access the birth path at the facilities designated to accommodate and follow up physiological pregnancy (see Rocca-Ihenacho & Alonso, 2020, for an in-depth discussion of the issue in the Covid-19 pandemic period).

The first visit should ideally take place by the 10th week of gestational age. The reception constitutes a fundamental moment of the path, as the woman can acquire important information that will allow her to make informed and conscious choices to better plan the care path she is about to take (Mselle et al., 2018). At the same time, the professional can ascertain the degree of risk of the pregnancy and decide with the woman on the most appropriate course of care (Healy et al., 2016; Sanders & Crozier, 2018). If the woman has been seen in the preconception phase, the specialist checks that the test reports are within the normal range; if not, the specialist will prescribe tests.

During the first meeting, the midwife completes the following steps in preparing the care plan:

- collects anamnestic information regarding past and current family, personal and obstetrical history, and lifestyle information;
- conducts a mental health history survey, paying special attention to any symptoms and signs of mental distress;
- checks the results of first trimester examinations or, if they have not yet been performed, prescribes them;
- provides the woman with all information about available services for care and support, proper nutrition, management of common symptoms in pregnancy, and screening;
- proceeds, together with the gynecologist, to assess the risk and identify the most appropriate course of action for the degree of risk identified (low, medium, or high);
- sets the date of the next appointment.

The gynecological specialist, based on the couple's family, personal, and obstetrical history, as well as the clinical examination and laboratory data, directs the woman to the care setting most appropriate to the identified risk profile (Figure 3.3).

3.4 Low-risk pregnancy pathway and medium-/high-risk pregnancy pathway

If the analysis performed reveals all the elements to consider the pregnancy as low-risk, according to the midwife-led continuity of care model (Alba et al., 2019; Hewitt et al., 2021; Mortensen et al., 2019) then the woman can be cared for entirely by the designated midwifery team and the woman's own midwife of record.

On the other hand, if the pregnancy shows signs or risk of maternal or fetal pathology, the woman is placed on the high-risk pathway (e.g., Ormesher et al., 2018). Some pregnancies, while not high-risk, require medical-specialist management and are considered "moderate risk" (Figure 3.4).

The birth path as a process: criticalities and cesarean section 45

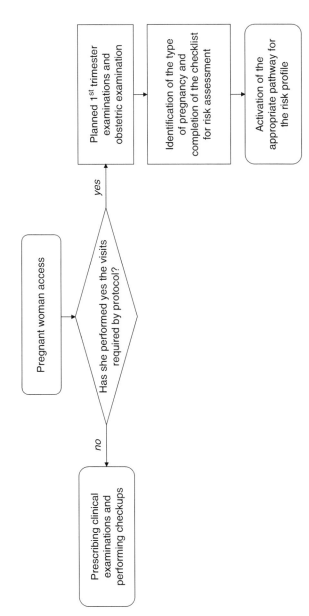

Figure 3.3 Access to the birth pathway phase.
Source: (authors' elaboration).

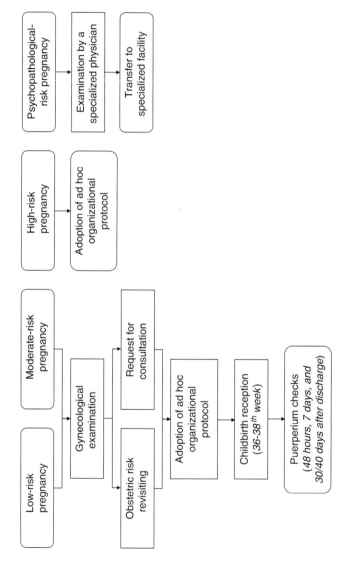

Figure 3.4 Low-risk pregnancy pathway and medium–/high-risk pregnancy pathway.
Source: (authors' elaboration).

This macro-process is based on the midwife-led continuity of care model. In this model, the central role is that of the midwife, who, drawing on the contributions of other professionals during pregnancy, birth, and puerperium, is committed to improving maternal and newborn health outcomes (Al-Mandhari et al., 2020; Crisp et al., 2018). This model of care can take a one-to-one or team-based midwifery care configuration. In the former case, a single midwife interfaces individually with each pregnant woman; in the latter case, each pregnant woman is managed in collaboration with other midwives (Sosa et al., 2018).

The "low-risk pregnancy" pathway consists of a series of scheduled meetings, during which the midwife:

- schedules examinations and ultrasounds;
- monitors that the pregnancy remains physiological;
- detects the possible occurrence of risk elements and, in that case, he/she reports the situation to the team's gynecologist in order to carry out all the necessary investigations, modifying the process and entrusting the woman to medical management.

Although pregnancy is a natural event for the woman's body, various factors can alter the normal course of gestation, creating dangers that can seriously compromise the health or life of the mother, the fetus, or both. In such a case, the woman enters the "high-risk pregnancy" or "psycho-pathological risk pregnancy" pathway, for which multidisciplinary care in centers of high care complexity is required.

3.5 Labor and delivery[1]

The woman's or couple's choice of birth point usually follows the logic of territorial proximity (Broda et al., 2018; Dickson et al., 2016; Kifle et al., 2018; Lambek, 2020). Only in some cases does the clinical situation of the woman or the fetus recommend that the delivery take place in facilities with Level II specialty care for the woman and neonatal intensive care for the unborn child (Figure 3.5).

At 36 weeks gestational age, the woman should access the chosen birth point for delivery (i.e., the checkup) regardless of the setting in which she was cared for during pregnancy. The checkup is an opportunity for the woman and the couple to visit the facility, learn about the access procedures and reception organization, ascertain whether the birth point meets the expectations and preferences accrued during the pregnancy, and familiarize themselves with the place where their baby will be born.

Intake procedures are aimed at identifying risk conditions for labor and delivery (World Health Organization, 2018). Depending on whether an obstetrical risk is present or not, labor and delivery are delegated to the care of the midwife in the case of physiological labor and delivery or to

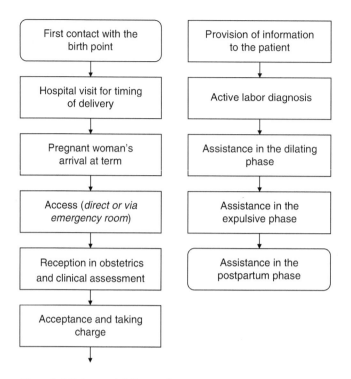

Figure 3.5 Labor and delivery phase.
Source: (authors' elaboration).

the physician together with the midwife in the case of pathological labor and delivery.

The midwife monitors the patient to determine whether labor has started so as to accompany her to the delivery room by coordinating the intake. She welcomes her to the labor room and follows the entire evolution of labor by supporting the woman so that labor remains in the physiological dimension.

The first stage of labor involves the diagnosis of active labor, which is formalized with the compilation of the partogram, which is then compiled with reference to the entire labor (Manjulatha et al., 2016). The second stage of labor begins with the achievement of full cervical dilation and ends with the expulsion of the fetus (Juhasova et al., 2018). Finally, the third stage of labor includes the period between the expulsion of the fetus and the fetal adnexa (placenta and membranes) (Serrano & Ayres-de-Campos, 2021).

Immediately after fetal expulsion, the midwife places the intrapartum blood loss control bag under the patient's pelvis (see Quibel et al., 2016). The disposable graduated bags should be maintained throughout the period of secondment until the patient leaves the delivery bed and before vulvar lavage. The amount of blood is easily measured on the graduated scale of the bag and should be reported on the medical record under "postpartum hemorrhage" (Sentilhes et al., 2016). Risk factors for postpartum hemorrhage are: fibromatous uterus, stage I labor greater than 24h, prolongation of stage III labor, pluriparity, fetal macrosomia, instrumental delivery, placenta previa, precipitous delivery, polyhydramnios, hypertension, obesity, uterine infection, and multiple pregnancy (Bienstock et al., 2021; Ende et al., 2021; Liu et al., 2021; Nyfløt et al., 2017). Nevertheless, hemorrhage can also occur in women who do not have these risk factors, so it is advisable that the staff present in the delivery room be adequately trained to deal with this type of complication. In the event of postpartum hemorrhage, they must perform a careful review of the birth canal to reveal any vulvo-vaginal or cervical lacerations and, if present, provide suturing. The obstetrician, on the other hand, is responsible for cannulating the vein, initiating infusion therapy, and drawing blood. If bleeding stops, close observation should be performed; if bleeding persists, the physician should call for further examination and possibly intervention.

If labor and delivery proceed without complications, delayed cord clamping and skin-to-skin contact are performed (Pacheco-Y Orozco et al., 2021; Widström et al., 2019); healthcare workers avoid washing the infants and refer them to the care of pediatricians immediately after birth only in case of complications. Today, numerous studies in the literature have shown that delayed umbilical cord clamping is associated with improved neonatal hemoglobin levels between 24 and 48 hours of life, improved iron stores between 3 and 6 months of age, and improved neurodevelopmental indices up to 4 years of age (Ashish et al., 2017; Marrs & Niermeyer, 2022). Furthermore, these benefits have been shown to be even more significant in pre-term births (Li et al., 2021; Peberdy et al., 2022; Prachukthum et al., 2022; Surak & Elsayed, 2022).

After the delivery is over, the patient is taken to a room where the midwife continues to assist her until discharge. Activities include regular checks in the first three hours postpartum; practicing lavage to safeguard the patient's intimate hygiene; checking blood and serum lochiae; performing therapy consisting of uterotonics, vitamins, snf antibiotics (if needed); and performing blood chemistry checks.

In the case of "elective/programmed" cesarean section (see Kamel & Thilaganathan, 2020) that has been preselected before the end of gestation, the patient is not transferred to the labor room but is accompanied directly to the operating block.

3.6 Puerperium

The puerperium phase is the period beginning immediately after childbirth and ending with the return of the female genital apparatus to its normal function (Rani & Ayyavoo, 2016; Weeks, 2017). Conventionally, a duration of 6 weeks is assigned to this period (Martínez-Galiano et al., 2019) (Figure 3.6).

50 *Gabriella Piscopo and Margherita Ruberto*

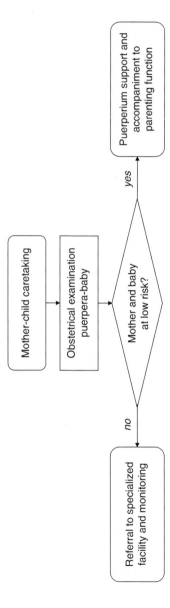

Figure 3.6 Puerperium phase.
Source: (authors' elaboration).

After delivery, the woman remains in the labor-partum room for the next two hours, during which the mother and infant practice skin-to-skin contact, a procedure that restores the infant's body temperature and stimulates early attachment to the breast (Kahalon et al., 2021; Spatz, 2022). During this period, the following steps are performed: checking the state of contracture of the uterus, checking for blood loss, checking the external genitalia, and taking vital signs.

At the end of two hours, if the postpartum course is physiological, the woman is accompanied to the ward and the infant is transferred to the nursery, unless rooming in is practiced in the facility. If conditions are favorable, the physician may discharge the woman usually after 48 hours in the case of spontaneous delivery or after 3–4 days if delivery was by cesarean section, but with precise reference to company procedures.

At the time of discharge, a report on the care received at the birth point is given to the woman. All this information will be needed by territorial facilities to ensure continuity of care, puerperium support, and accompaniment to parenthood.

3.7 Cesarean section and medicalization of pregnancy

Empirical evidence and scientific research (e.g., Brites et al., 2020; Najmabadi et al., 2020; Ranjbar et al., 2019) show that the most problematic aspect of the childbirth event is the trend, observed in recent years, toward medicalization of birth. This trend negatively influences the birth path by impacting, in particular, access to the pregnancy pathway and the actual moment of childbirth.

The fact that arouses the most attention in the scientific and institutional community is the high incidence of cesarean section recorded beyond cases of high-risk pregnancy (Jafarzadeh et al., 2019; Rasool et al., 2021).

Indeed, it is precisely the frequency of cesarean sections that represents one of the quality indicators used internationally to assess progress in maternal and child health. Therefore, the phenomenon has been the subject of extensive discussion within the different disciplinary areas pertaining to both the clinical and the managerial and health policy areas. The pursuit of models capable of ensuring an appropriate management strategy for childbirth continues to be of crucial importance (Betran et al., 2018).

Cesarean section is a surgical intervention that can reduce maternal and perinatal mortality and morbidity when performed on the basis of a specific medical indication. This intervention remains uncommon in some low-development countries but has become overused in many parts of the world. The primary interest of this study is not the benefits of cesarean section in regions where it is underutilized but the effects of its increasing use (Bernitz et al., 2019). Indeed, many studies have shown that rates of cesarean sections above a certain limit do not show additional benefits (e.g., Chen et al., 2018; Keag et al., 2018). In addition, like any surgical procedure, it is not without risk, as it can compromise the health of the woman, the baby, and future pregnancies due to mid- and long-term complications (Sandall et al., 2018).

The exponential increase in cesarean section has received much attention from the World Health Organization, which convened a committee of international reproductive health experts in Brazil in 1985 to discuss the phenomenon. The panel of experts formulated its hypotheses based on the scant data available, derived from studies conducted mostly in northern European countries with maternal and perinatal mortality among the lowest in the world. From that important moment of analysis came the conclusion that the ideal cesarean section rate should be between 10% and 15% of all births (Betrán et al., 2016; Kanji et al., 2019; World Health Organization, 2015).

Although these rates have been determined to be optimal by the international community, there have been increases in cesarean section rates in both developed and developing countries over the past three decades (Ganeriwal et al., 2021). As a result, there is increased concern about the negative health consequences for mothers and children (Chen & Tan, 2019; Keag et al., 2018), as well as the burden that cesarean sections may place on healthcare spending (Cunningham et al., 2017; Hoxha & Fink, 2021; Moran et al., 2020; Sobhy et al., 2019).

In 2014, the WHO convened the expert committee again in Geneva to revise the recommended rate by conducting the analysis again on more current data. The analysis conducted by WHO found that:

1 cesarean sections are effective in reducing maternal and infant mortality only if performed on strict medical indication;
2 at the population level, the cesarean section rate is recognized as functional in reducing maternal and infant mortality only if it is contained within the limits of 15%, while above this threshold no reduction in mortality can be found;
3 the cesarean section rate may be correlated with increased risks when the care conditions and infrastructure are not sufficient to ensure safe intervention;
4 women should only be subjected to cesarean section only if there is a medical need, regardless of the target rate.

However, although the healthcare delivery system has improved over the years in terms of efficiency and accessibility, the cesarean section rate has not been reduced (Ganeriwal et al., 2021). Rates recommended based on data obtained from population studies cannot be considered truly ideal, as they are not expressive of the real potential and capacity of individual healthcare facilities. In fact, within the different geographical and sociocultural contexts, the use of cesarean section is also influenced by other factors, such as organizational structure, availability of financial and operational resources, protocols used, and the different composition of the population (Schantz et al., 2019; Sindiani et al., 2020).

Table 3.1 Robson's classification

Class 1	Nulliparous mothers, single fetus, cephalic presentation, at term (gestational age ≥37 weeks), spontaneous labor
Class 2a	Nulliparous mothers, single fetus, cephalic presentation, at term (gestational age ≥37 weeks), induced labor
Class 2b	Nulliparous mothers, single fetus, cephalic presentation, at term (gestational age ≥37 weeks), CT scan before labor
Class 3	Multiparous mothers (no previous CT), single fetus, cephalic presentation, at term (gestational age ≥37 weeks), spontaneous labor
Class 4a	Multiparous mothers (no previous CT), single fetus, cephalic presentation, at term (gestational age ≥37 weeks), induced labor
Class 4b	Multiparous mothers (no previous CT), single fetus, cephalic presentation, at term (gestational age ≥37 weeks), CT before labor
Class 5	Previous CT, single fetus, cephalic presentation, at term (gestational age ≥37 weeks)
Class 6	Nulliparous mothers, single fetus, breech presentation
Class 7	Multiparous mothers (including women with previous CT), single fetus, breech presentation
Class 8	Multiple pregnancies (including women with previous CT scan)
Class 9	Single fetus, abnormal presentation (including women with previous CT); Class 10: pre-term delivery (gestational age ≤36 weeks), single fetus, breech presentation (including women with previous CT)

To meet local and international needs for monitoring and comparing cesarean section rates in one hospital facility, among different hospital facilities, and in different referral populations, WHO decided to use Robson's Classification system (Table 3.1) as a global standard, according to which each woman at the time of admission for childbirth is classified into one of 10 groups on the basis of 5 obstetrical characteristics (Robson et al., 2015):

1 parity (nulliparous, multiparous with or without previous cesarean section);
2 mode of labor onset (spontaneous, induced, or cesarean section in absence of labor);
3 gestational age (preterm, full-term);
4 fetal presentation (cephalic, breech, or transverse);
5 number of fetuses (single or multiple pregnancy).

Although Robson's classification constitutes a clear and shared reference standard, the incidence of cesarean sections presents empirical evidence such that it does not allow exclusive association with determinants of a clinical nature. Indeed, the phenomenon under investigation is affected by the influence of a multiplicity of variables of different nature. For example, uncertainty about what the vaginal birth will be like (e.g., how much pain it will cause) and good opinions of CS are all main causes of women's preference for cesarean delivery (Colomar et al., 2021).

The clinical and managerial scientific literature identifies seven macro-categories covering all factors of variation in CT rates, as described below.

3.7.1 Known medical risk factors

Studies show that deliveries with surgical intervention performed without medical necessity, especially in low-resource settings, are associated with risks and complications for the mother, the baby, and subsequent pregnancies (Declercq et al., 2007; Liu et al., 2007; Sanchez-Ramos et al., 2001; Souza et al., 2010).

In particular, neonatal complications include respiratory distress, low APGAR score, fetal injury, allergic rhinitis, food allergy, infant asthma, and infantile onset of type 1 diabetes (Bager et al., 2008; Domingues et al., 2021; Thavagnanam et al., 2008), while maternal complications include increased likelihood of maternal mortality, blood transfusions, hysterectomy, increased risk of infection, transfusion complications, fistulae, cardiac arrest, admission to the intensive care unit, increased recovery time, medication reactions, and risk of postpartum depression (Ahmeidat et al., 2021; Cho & Jeong, 2021; Kallianidis et al., 2018; Larsson et al., 2021; Pereira et al., 2019; Sandall et al., 2018; Torkan et al., 2009).

According to Degani and Sikich (2015) it is possible to distinguish maternal, infant, and obstetric risk factors that affect the likelihood of cesarean delivery:

- maternal factors: age, pre-existing health conditions (diabetes, obesity, hypertension, previous cesarean delivery, pregnancy-related health conditions including gestational diabetes), pre-eclampsia, eclampsia;
- infant factors: prenatal problems preceding the intrapartum period (such as fetal abnormalities and/or intrauterine growth restriction) and suspected macrosomia, malposition, or multiple births;
- obstetric factors: placental abruption, placenta accreta, placenta previa, prolapse of the heart cord, and nonreassuring fetal heart trace.

3.7.2 Social and demographic factors

According to several studies in the literature, the observed changes in women's reproductive behavior play a leading role in the excessive increase in cesarean section rates – relating to factors attributable to nonmedical reasons.

An association has been found between advanced maternal age and the use of cesarean section practice (Bayrampour et al., 2012; Klemetti et al., 2016; Mastina & Murdani, 2019; Montori et al., 2021; Richards et al., 2016; Rydahl et al., 2019; Walker & Thornton, 2021). Advanced maternal age is also associated with prenatal, intrapartum, and postpartum problems, such as miscarriage, preeclampsia (Waldenström & Ekéus, 2017), gestational diabetes (Timofeev et al., 2013), placenta previa (Mohammadi et al., 2016), assisted conception, preterm delivery, fetal chromosomal abnormalities, low birth weight, stillbirth, and multiple births (Ankarcrona et al., 2019).

In addition to advanced maternal age, other social and demographic factors associated with cesarean section are reported in the literature, including high maternal education level, high income level, and residence in an urban area (e.g., Kizito, 2021; Mose & Abebe, 2021). Moreover, a very relevant factor in this area is consultation with relatives (Bam et al., 2021), which influences the choice of cesarean delivery more than the baby's life risk or history of previous CS; however, this is a complex and multi-faced demographic issue (Jatta et al., 2021).

According to some studies, older age is correlated with greater preference for elective cesarean delivery (Fuma et al., 2019; Kjerulff et al., 2019); in addition, women with higher (vs. lower) education appear more likely to prefer a primary cesarean section (Dweik et al., 2014). Finally, the impact of socioeconomic variables (regular household income and occupation) on cesarean delivery is also significant (Berglundh et al., 2021; Kizito, 2021).

3.7.3 Professional practice styles factors

Many factors affect the physician's assessment of whether a cesarean section should be performed. Different medical practices lead to assessing clinical conditions differently, so a risk-averse physician may decide to resort to cesarean section to avoid any type of error (Fuglenes et al., 2009; López-López et al., 2021; Murray et al., 2007; Smith et al., 2021). A fundamental aspect to evaluate is the use of defensive medicine, which pushes physicians to focus less on what is right and appropriate than on what protects them from the risk of litigation (Mushinski et al., 2021; Rudey et al., 2021).

The physician's decision is also strongly influenced by financial incentives, cultural factors, organizational factors, lack of experience, and progressive loss of information about childbirth (Bailit, 2012; Epstein, 2009; Grant, 2005; Habiba et al., 2006; Litorp et al., 2015; Shirzad et al., 2021; Zwecker et al., 2011).

3.7.4 Factors influencing maternal decision-making

Analysis of the literature finds that the use of cesarean sections is also linked to an increase in maternal demands (Begum et al., 2021; Loke et al., 2015; Parikh & Pandya, 2021; Reyes & Rosenberg, 2019; Schantz et al., 2021).

Women's preferences for mode of birth are influenced by a number of personal, cultural, and social factors (Topçu, 2021). In general, information and/or misinformation from the facility can influence women's choices (Coates et al., 2021). Women prefer to undergo a cesarean section because they perceive a number of advantages over vaginal delivery; for example, it avoids labor pain, reduces the risk of urinary incontinence, and minimizes sexual dissatisfaction after delivery (Stoll et al., 2017).

3.7.5 Organizational factors

Other factors that strongly affect the use of cesarean section are attributable to structural and organizational deficiencies in healthcare facilities, poor training of healthcare personnel in providing appropriate care in the delivery room, lack of expertise in managing complicated natural deliveries, and the mistaken belief that cesarean section is safer. The latter can occur because of doctors' failure to communicate or misinformation patients obtain from other sources (Doraiswamy et al., 2021; Otieno & Akwala, 2021; Shetty et al., 2021).

The choice of cesarean section is influenced, therefore, by organizational practices that differ among hospitals. In many facilities, there is an absence of useful services to promote spontaneous childbirth (Nyamtema et al., 2021). In fact, while many women are able to cope with the anxieties and fears associated with childbirth, others are frightened of pain and view it as an enemy to be eliminated (Webb et al., 2021). Taking advantage of the continuous peridural analgesia technique, when available, makes it possible to control the pain while giving birth spontaneously (Imarengiaye, 2021; Keita et al., 2021).

In addition, facilities should be equipped with rooms to perform water birth, a modality that promotes natural childbirth by offering numerous benefits for both the woman and the newborn such as: decrease in pain (through natural analgesia), decrease in the duration of labor, reduction in the incidence of perineal trauma, reduction in the use of drugs, and reduction in the incidence of operative deliveries (Bartlett, 2017; Cluett et al., 2018; Estuardo et al., 2021; Poder & Larivière, 2014).

Finally, recent studies in the literature (e.g., Hailemeskel et al., 2021; Mortensen et al., 2019; Rayment-Jones et al., 2021) have found that midwife-led continuity of care models improve maternal and newborn health outcomes. In fact, the benefit of being cared for during pregnancy is related to receiving more information, better instruction, increased confidence, and greater empowerment. Women who received more information from midwives during pregnancy have less risk of induction of labor, the overuse of which increases the risk of uterine rupture, perinatal trauma, and anal sphincter damage (Baxter, 2021; Miller et al., 2016).

3.7.6 Economic factors

According to the prevailing literature, economic determinants also strongly influence the increase in cesarean section rates worldwide. Many studies attribute this increase to financial incentives by healthcare providers, because most healthcare systems involve different reimbursements for the two delivery modalities (Hoxha & Fink, 2021). In particular, cesarean section, being a surgical procedure, is reimbursed more than vaginal delivery, which is a medical procedure (Berta et al., 2019; Cavalieri et al., 2014; Henderson et al., 2001; Tadevosyan et al., 2019).

There is general agreement in the literature that cesarean sections consume more hospital resources than vaginal deliveries because they require the performance of more activities and the involvement of a greater number of employed staff, more equipment and consumables, greater consumption of drugs, and longer hospital stays (see Negrini et al., 2021).

Thus, according to several studies, financial incentives occupy a key role in increasing the rates of cesarean sections by pushing hospitals to perform more cesarean sections as a more profitable mode of delivery (Hoxha & Fink, 2021). Under the fee system, all hospitals are reimbursed through a flat fee for each Diagnosis Related Group (DRG). Sometimes there is an additional payment for patients with extremely long stays or excessively prohibitive costs.

The difference in payment incentivizes healthcare facilities to require unnecessary procedures, thereby changing the behavior of physicians, who shift demand in the direction of their own interests (Allin et al., 2015; Grant, 2009; Kim et al., 2016; Litorp et al., 2015).

3.7.7 Cultural factors

Culture plays a key role in decision making; in many cases, personal beliefs, social influences, religious orientation, and even false beliefs guide decisions and modify behavior (Coates et al., 2021; Djatmika et al., 2021; Hou et al., 2014; Karlström et al., 2011; Kornelsen et al., 2010; Orji et al., 2003).

Some personal beliefs stem from experiences related to previous pregnancies or are influenced by others' experiences (Sanavi et al., 2012; Schantz et al., 2021). In many cultures, childbirth is associated with anxieties and fears that give childbirth a negative connotation, prompting women to consider a cesarean section as less painful, safer, and less likely to negatively affect the quality of sexual life (Leeman & Rogers, 2012; Olaru et al., 2021; Sahlin et al., 2021). Conversely, other women have a positive perception of vaginal birth, as they consider it a natural process associated with a faster recovery (Domingues et al., 2021). In some cases, women are convinced that they must give birth by cesarean section because they have undergone surgery in their previous pregnancy (McGrath et al., 2010).

The decision to opt for a cesarean section is often influenced by pressure from partners, family, friends, and the media (Fenwick et al., 2010; Hull et al., 2011; Roy et al., 2021; Tohid, 2011). Popular beliefs, such as perceived advantages for the baby to be born on a specific date, also have an impact in some contexts. This aspect is also related to the fact that many working women want to be able to decide what day to give birth and thus organize their professional activity accordingly (Huang et al., 2013; Pang et al., 2008).

Note

1 Edited by Paola De Rosa, Midwife, University Hospital of Parma, Parma, Italy.

References

Ahmeidat, A., Kotts, W. J., Wong, J., McLernon, D. J., & Black, M. (2021). Predictive models of individual risk of elective caesarean section complications: a systematic review. *European Journal of Obstetrics & Gynecology and Reproductive Biology*, *262*, 248–255.

Al-Mandhari, A., Gedik, F. G., Mataria, A., Oweis, A., & Hajjeh, R. (2020). 2020–the year of the nurse and midwife: a call for action to scale up and strengthen the nursing and midwifery workforce in the Eastern Mediterranean Region. *Eastern Mediterranean Health Journal*, *26*(4), 370–371.

Alba, R., Franco, R., Patrizia, B., Maria, C. B., Giovanna, A., Chiara, F., & Isabella, N. (2019). The midwifery-led care model: a continuity of care model in the birth path. *Acta Bio Medica: Atenei Parmensis*, *90*(Suppl 6), 41.

Allin, S., Baker, M., Isabelle, M., & Stabile, M. (2015). *Physician incentives and the rise in c-sections: evidence from Canada* (No. 21022). National Bureau of Economic Research, Inc.

Ankarcrona, V., Altman, D., Wikström, A. K., Jacobsson, B., & Brismar Wendel, S. (2019). Delivery outcome after trial of labor in nulliparous women 40 years or older—A nationwide population-based study. *Acta Obstetricia et Gynecologica Scandinavica*, *98*(9), 1195–1203.

Ashish, K. C., Rana, N., Målqvist, M., Ranneberg, L. J., Subedi, K., & Andersson, O. (2017). Effects of delayed umbilical cord clamping vs early clamping on anemia in infants at 8 and 12 months: a randomized clinical trial. *JAMA Pediatrics*, *171*(3), 264–270.

Bager, P., Wohlfahrt, J., & Westergaard, T. (2008). Caesarean delivery and risk of atopy and allergic disesase: meta-analyses. *Clinical & Experimental Allergy*, *38*(4), 634–642.

Bagheri, A., Masoodi-Alavi, N., & Abbaszade, F. (2012). Effective factors for choosing the delivery method among the pregnant women in Kashan. *KAUMS Journal (FEYZ)*, *16*(2), 146–153.

Bailit, J. (2012). Impact of non-clinical factors on primary cesarean deliveries. *Semin Perinatol*, *36*, 395–398.

Bam, V., Lomotey, A. Y., Diji, A. K. A., Budu, H. I., Bamfo-Ennin, D., & Mireku, G. (2021). Factors influencing decision-making to accept elective caesarean section: a descriptive cross-sectional study. *Heliyon*, *7*(8), e07755.

Bartlett, J. (2017). Water birth in the hospital setting. *International Journal of Childbirth Education*, *32*(2).

Baxter, E. (2021). A midwifery-led prevalence programme for caesarean section surgical site infections. *Journal of Hospital Infection*, *109*, 78–81.

Bayrampour, H., Heaman, M., Duncan, K. A., & Tough, S. (2012). Advanced maternal age and risk perception: a qualitative study. *BMC Pregnancy and Childbirth*, *12*(1), 100.

Begum, T., Saif-Ur-Rahman, K. M., Yaqoot, F., Stekelenburg, J., Anuradha, S., Biswas, T., … & Mamun, A. A. (2021). Global incidence of caesarean deliveries on maternal request: a systematic review and meta-regression. *BJOG: An International Journal of Obstetrics & Gynaecology*, *128*(5), 798–806.

Berglundh, S., Benova, L., Olisaekee, G., & Hanson, C. (2021). Caesarean section rate in Nigeria between 2013 and 2018 by obstetric risk and socio-economic status. *Tropical Medicine & International Health*, 26(7), 775–788.

Bernitz, S., Dalbye, R., Zhang, J., Eggebø, T. M., Frøslie, K. F., Olsen, I. C., ... & Øian, P. (2019). The frequency of intrapartum caesarean section use with the WHO partograph versus Zhang's guideline in the Labour Progression Study (LaPS): a multicentre, cluster-randomised controlled trial. *The Lancet*, 393(10169), 340–348.

Berta, P., Martini, G., Piacenza, M., & Turati, G. (2019). *The strange case of appropriate C-sections: DRG-tariff regulation, hospital ownership, and market concentration*. HEDG, c/o Department of Economics, University of York.

Betran, A. P., Temmerman, M., Kingdon, C., Mohiddin, A., Opiyo, N., Torloni, M. R., ... & Downe, S. (2018). Interventions to reduce unnecessary caesarean sections in healthy women and babies. *The Lancet*, 392(10155), 1358–1368.

Betrán, A. P., Torloni, M. R., Zhang, J. J., Gülmezoglu, A. M., Aleem, H. A., Althabe, F., ... & Zongo, A. (2016). WHO statement on caesarean section rates. *Bjog*, 123(5), 667.

Bienstock, J. L., Eke, A. C., & Hueppchen, N. A. (2021). Postpartum hemorrhage. *New England Journal of Medicine*, 384(17), 1635–1645.

Brites, R., Nunes, O., Pires, M., & Hipólito, J. (2020). The subjective experience of pregnancy and the expectations of childbirth on a medicalized world: a qualitative study. *The Psychologist: Practice & Research Journal*, 3(1), 1–9.

Broda, A., Krüger, J., Schinke, S., & Weber, A. (2018). Determinants of choice of delivery place: testing rational choice theory and habitus theory. *Midwifery*, 63, 33–38.

Cavalieri, M., Guccio, C., Lisi, D., & Pignataro, G. (2014). Financial incentives and in-appropriateness in health care: evidence from Italian cesarean sections. *FinanzArchiv/Public Finance Analysis*, 70(3), 430–457.

Chen, I., Opiyo, N., Tavender, E., Mortazhejri, S., Rader, T., Petkovic, J., ... & Betran, A. P. (2018). Non-clinical interventions for reducing unnecessary caesarean section. *Cochrane Database of Systematic Reviews*, 9(9), CD005528. 10.1002/14651858.CD005528.pub3

Chen, H., & Tan, D. (2019). Cesarean section or natural childbirth? cesarean birth may damage your health. *Frontiers in Psychology*, 10, 351.

Cho, H., & Jeong, I. S. (2021). The relationship between mother-infant contact time and changes in postpartum depression and mother-infant attachment among mothers staying at postpartum care centers: an observational study. *Nursing & Health Sciences*, 23(2), 547–555.

Cluett, E. R., Burns, E., & Cuthbert, A. (2018). Immersion in water during labour and birth. *Cochrane Database of Systematic Reviews*, 5(5), CD000111. 10.1002/14651858.CD000111.pub4

Coates, D., Donnolley, N., Thirukumar, P., Lainchbury, A., Spear, V., & Henry, A. (2021). Women's experiences of decision-making and beliefs in relation to planned caesarean section: a survey study. *Australian and New Zealand Journal of Obstetrics and Gynaecology*, 61(1), 106–115.

Colomar, M., Opiyo, N., Kingdon, C., Long, Q., Nion, S., Bohren, M. A., & Betran, A. P. (2021). Do women prefer caesarean sections? A qualitative evidence synthesis of their views and experiences. *PLoS One*, 16(5), e0251072.

Crisp, N., Brownie, S., & Refsum, C. (2018). Nursing & midwifery: the key to the rapid and cost effective expansion of high quality universal healthcare. *Doha, Qatar, World Innovation Summit for Health*, 1–39.

Cunningham, S. D., Herrera, C., Udo, I. E., Kozhimannil, K. B., Barrette, E., Magriples, U., & Ickovics, J. R. (2017). Maternal medical complexity: impact on prenatal health care spending among women at low risk for cesarean section. *Women's Health Issues*, 27(5), 551–558.

Declercq, E., Barger, M., Cabral, H. J., Evans, S. R., Kotelchuck, M., Simon, C., ... & Heffner, L. J. (2007). Maternal outcomes associated with planned primary cesarean births compared with planned vaginal births. *Obstetrics & Gynecology*, 109(3), 669–677.

Degani, N., & Sikich, N. (2015). Caesarean delivery rate review: an evidence-based analysis. *Ontario Health Technology Assessment Series*, 15(9), 1.

Dickson, K. S., Adde, K. S., & Amu, H. (2016). What influences where they give birth? Determinants of place of delivery among women in rural Ghana. *International Journal of Reproductive Medicine*, 2016, 7203980. 10.1155/2016/7203980

Djatmika, C., Lusher, J., Meyrick, J., & Byron-Daniel, J. (2021). Caesarean section as an informed choice in the UK: a systematic review. *British Journal of Midwifery*, 29(10), 579–588.

Domingues, R. M. S. M., Luz, P. M., da Silva Ayres, B. V., Torres, J. A., & do Carmo Leal, M. (2021). Cost-effectiveness analysis of a quality improvement program to reduce caesarean sections in Brazilian private hospitals: a case study. *Reproductive Health*, 18(1), 1–13.

Doraiswamy, S., Billah, S. M., Karim, F., Siraj, M. S., Buckingham, A., & Kingdon, C. (2021). Physician–patient communication in decision-making about caesarean sections in eight district hospitals in Bangladesh: a mixed-method study. *Reproductive health*, 18(1), 1–14.

Dweik, D., Girasek, E., Mészáros, G., Töreki, A., Keresztúri, A., & Pál, A. (2014). Non-medical determinants of cesarean section in a medically dominated maternity system. *Acta Obstetricia et Gynecologica Scandinavica*, 93(10), 1025–1033.

Ende, H. B., Lozada, M. J., Chestnut, D. H., Osmundson, S. S., Walden, R. L., Shotwell, M. S., & Bauchat, J. R. (2021). Risk factors for atonic postpartum hemorrhage: a systematic review and meta-analysis. *Obstetrics and Gynecology*, 137(2), 305.

Epstein, A. J., & Nicholson, S. (2009). The formation and evolution of physician treatment styles: an application to cesarean sections. *Journal of Health Economics*, 28(6), 1126–1140.

Estuardo, L. I. J., Carlos, D. M., Roberto, H. R., de Jesús, Á. P. F., Jorge, S. M., Antonio, Y. G. M., ... & Manuel, V. H. V. (2021). Delivery in water, experience in a population of Mexican women in Mexico City. *Journal of Gynecological Research and Obstetrics*, 7(3), 055–060.

Fenwick, J., Staff, L., Gamble, J., Creedy, D. K., & Bayes, S. (2010). Why do women request caesarean section in a normal, healthy first pregnancy?. *Midwifery*, 26(4), 394–400.

Fuglenes, D., Øian, P., & Kristiansen, I. S. (2009). Obstetricians' choice of cesarean delivery in ambiguous cases: is it influenced by risk attitude or fear of complaints and litigation? *American Journal of Obstetrics and Gynecology*, 200(1), 48–e1.

Fuma, K., Maseki, Y., Tezuka, A., Kuribayashi, M., Tsuda, H., & Furuhashi, M. (2019). Factors associated with intrapartum cesarean section in women aged 40 years or older: a single-center experience in Japan. *The Journal of Maternal-Fetal & Neonatal Medicine*, 34(2), 216–222. 10.1080/14767058.2019.1602601

Ganeriwal, S. A., Ryan, G. A., Purandare, N. C., & Purandare, C. N. (2021). Examining the role and relevance of the critical analysis and comparison of cesarean section rates in a changing world. *Taiwanese Journal of Obstetrics and Gynecology*, 60(1), 20–23.

Geller, S. E., Koch, A. R., Garland, C. E., MacDonald, E. J., Storey, F., & Lawton, B. (2018). A global view of severe maternal morbidity: moving beyond maternal mortality. *Reproductive Health*, 15(1), 31–43.

Grandi, S. M., Filion, K. B., Yoon, S., Ayele, H. T., Doyle, C. M., Hutcheon, J. A., ... & Platt, R. W. (2019). Cardiovascular disease-related morbidity and mortality in women with a history of pregnancy complications: systematic review and meta-analysis. *Circulation*, 139(8), 1069–1079.

Grant, D. (2005). Explaining source of payment differences in US cesarean rates: why do privately insured mothers receive more cesareans than mothers who are not privately insured? *Health Care Management Science*, 8(1), 5–17.

Grant, D. (2009). Physician financial incentives and cesarean delivery: new conclusions from the healthcare cost and utilization project. *Journal of Health Economics*, 28(1), 244–250.

Habiba, M., Kaminski, M., Da Fre, M., Marsal, K., Bleker, O., Librero, J., ... & Taylor, D. (2006). Caesarean section on request: a comparison of obstetricians' attitudes in eight European countries. *BJOG: An International Journal of Obstetrics & Gynaecology*, 113(6), 647–656.

Hailemeskel, S., Alemu, K., Christensson, K., Tesfahun, E., & Lindgren, H. (2021). Health care providers' perceptions and experiences related to Midwife-led continuity of care–a qualitative study. *PloS one*, 16(10), e0258248.

Healy, S., Humphreys, E., & Kennedy, C. (2016). Midwives' and obstetricians' perceptions of risk and its impact on clinical practice and decision-making in labour: an integrative review. *Women and Birth*, 29(2), 107–116.

Henderson, J., McCandlish, R., Kumiega, L., & Petrou, S. (2001). Systematic review of economic aspects of alternative modes of delivery. *BJOG: An International Journal of Obstetrics & Gynaecology*, 108(2), 149–157.

Hewitt, L., Dahlen, H. G., Hartz, D. L., & Dadich, A. (2021). Leadership and management in midwifery-led continuity of care models: a thematic and lexical analysis of a scoping review. *Midwifery*, 98, 102986.

Hou, X., Rakhshani, N. S., & Iunes, R. (2014). Factors associated with high Cesarean deliveries in China and Brazil-A Call for reducing elective surgeries in moving towards Universal Health Coverage. *Journal of Hospital Administration*, 3(5), 67–78.

Hoxha, I., & Fink, G. (2021). Caesarean sections and health financing: a global analysis. *BMJ Open*, 11(5), e044383.

Huang, S. Y., Sheu, S. J., Tai, C. J., Chiang, C. P., & Chien, L. Y. (2013). Decision-making process for choosing an elective cesarean delivery among primiparas in Taiwan. *Maternal and Child Health Journal*, 17(5), 842–851.

Hull, P. M., Bedwell, C., & Lavender, T. (2011). Why do some women prefer birth by caesarean? An internet survey. *British Journal of Midwifery*, 19(11), 708–717.

Imarengiaye, C. (2021). Obstetrical Analgesia and Anaesthesia. In *Contemporary Obstetrics and Gynecology for Developing Countries* (pp. 223–233). Cham: Springer.

Jafarzadeh, A., Hadavi, M., Hassanshahi, G., Rezaeian, M., Vazirinejad, R., Aminzadeh, F., & Sarkoohi, A. (2019). Cesarean or cesarean epidemic?. *Archives of Iranian Medicine (AIM)*, 22(11).

Jatta, F., Sundby, J., Vangen, S., Lindskog, B. V., Sørbye, I. K., & Owe, K. M. (2021). Association between maternal origin, pre-pregnancy body mass index and caesarean section: a nation-wide registry study. *International Journal of Environmental Research and Public Health*, *18*(11), 5938.

Juhasova, J., Kreft, M., Zimmermann, R., & Kimmich, N. (2018). Impact factors on cervical dilation rates in the first stage of labor. *Journal of Perinatal Medicine*, *46*(1), 59–66.

Kahalon, R., Preis, H., & Benyamini, Y. (2021). Who benefits most from skin-to-skin mother-infant contact after birth? Survey findings on skin-to-skin and birth satisfaction by mode of birth. *Midwifery*, *92*, 102862.

Kanji, Z., Simonovich, S. D., Najmi, N., & Bishop-Royse, J. (2019). Examining clinical indications for cesarean section in a university hospital in Karachi, Pakistan. *Journal of Asian Midwives (JAM)*, *6*(1), 14–25.

Karlström, A., Nystedt, A., Johansson, M., & Hildingsson, I. (2011). Behind the myth–few women prefer caesarean section in the absence of medical or obstetrical factors. *Midwifery*, *27*(5), 620–627.

Keita, H., Deruelle, P., Bouvet, L., Bonnin, M., Chassard, D., Bouthors, A. S., ... & Benhamou, D. (2021). Raising awareness to prevent, recognise and manage acute pain during caesarean delivery: the French Practice Bulletin. *Anaesthesia Critical Care & Pain Medicine*, *40*(5), 100934.

Klemetti, R., Gissler, M., Sainio, S., & Hemminki, E. (2016). At what age does the risk for adverse maternal and infant outcomes increase? Nationwide register-based study on first births in Finland in 2005–2014. *Acta Obstetricia et Gynecologica Scandinavica*, *95*(12), 1368–1375.

Kornelsen, J., Hutton, E., & Munro, S. (2010). Influences on decision making among primiparous women choosing elective caesarean section in the absence of medical indications: findings from a qualitative investigation. *Journal of Obstetrics and Gynaecology Canada*, *32*(10), 962–969.

Kallianidis, A. F., Schutte, J. M., Van Roosmalen, J., & Van Den Akker, T. (2018). Maternal mortality after cesarean section in the Netherlands. *European Journal of Obstetrics & Gynecology and Reproductive Biology*, *229*, 148–152.

Kamel, R., & Thilaganathan, B. (2020). Time to reconsider elective Cesarean birth. *Ultrasound in Obstetrics & Gynecology*, *57*(3), 363–365.

Keag, O. E., Norman, J. E., & Stock, S. J. (2018). Long-term risks and benefits associated with cesarean delivery for mother, baby, and subsequent pregnancies: systematic review and meta-analysis. *PLoS Medicine*, *15*(1), e1002494.

Kifle, M. M., Kesete, H. F., Gaim, H. T., Angosom, G. S., & Araya, M. B. (2018). Health facility or home delivery? Factors influencing the choice of delivery place among mothers living in rural communities of Eritrea. *Journal of Health, Population and Nutrition*, *37*(1), 1–15.

Kim, S. J., Han, K. T., Kim, S. J., Park, E. C., & Park, H. K. (2016). Impact of a diagnosis-related group payment system on cesarean section in Korea. *Health Policy*, *120*(6), 596–603.

Kizito, O. (2021). Determinants of caesarean section rates in private-not-for-profit healthcare facilities: St. Joseph's Hospital_ Kitovu. *Cogent Medicine*, *8*(1), 1928939.

Kjerulff, K. H., Attanasio, L. B., Edmonds, J. K., & Repke, J. T. (2019). Mode of delivery preference among pregnant nulliparous women. *Journal of Women's Health*, *28*(6), 874–884.

Kozhimannil, K. B., Interrante, J. D., Tofte, A. N., & Admon, L. K. (2020). Severe maternal morbidity and mortality among indigenous women in the United States. *Obstetrics and gynecology*, *135*(2), 294.

Lambek, M. (2020). How do women give birth?. In *Questions of Anthropology* (pp. 197–225). Routledge.

Larsson, C., Djuvfelt, E., Lindam, A., Tunón, K., & Nordin, P. (2021). Surgical complications after caesarean section: a population-based cohort study. *PloS One*, *16*(10), e0258222.

Leeman, L. M., & Rogers, R. G. (2012). Sex after childbirth: postpartum sexual function. *Obstetrics & Gynecology*, *119*(3), 647–655.

Litorp, H., Mgaya, A., Mbekenga, C. K., Kidanto, H. L., Johnsdotter, S., & Essén, B. (2015). Fear, blame and transparency: obstetric caregivers' rationales for high caesarean section rates in a low-resource setting. *Social Science & Medicine*, *143*, 232–240.

Liu, S., Liston, R. M., Joseph, K. S., Heaman, M., Sauve, R., & Kramer, M. S. (2007). Maternal mortality and severe morbidity associated with low-risk planned cesarean delivery versus planned vaginal delivery at term. *CMAJ*, *176*(4), 455–460.

Liu, C. N., Yu, F. B., Xu, Y. Z., Li, J. S., Guan, Z. H., Sun, M. N., ... & Chen, D. J. (2021). Prevalence and risk factors of severe postpartum hemorrhage: a retrospective cohort study. *BMC Pregnancy and Childbirth*, *21*(1), 1–8.

Loke, A. Y., Davies, L., & Li, S. F. (2015). Factors influencing the decision that women make on their mode of delivery: the Health Belief Model. *BMC Health Services Research*, *15*(1), 274.

López-López, A. I., Sanz-Valero, J., Gómez-Pérez, L., & Pastor-Valero, M. (2021). Pelvic floor: vaginal or caesarean delivery? A review of systematic reviews. *International Urogynecology Journal*, *32*(7), 1663–1673.

Löwy, I. (2017). *Imperfect pregnancies: a history of birth defects and prenatal diagnosis*. JHU Press.

Manjulatha, V. R., Anitha, G. S., & Shivalingaiah, N. (2016). Partogram: clinical study to assess the role of Partogram in primigravidae in labor. *International Journal of Reproduction, Contraception, Obstetrics and Gynecology*, *5*(4), 1014–1026.

Marrs, L., & Niermeyer, S. (2022). Toward greater nuance in delayed cord clamping. *Current Opinion in Pediatrics*, *34*(2), 170–177.

Martínez-Galiano, J. M., Hernández-Martínez, A., Rodríguez-Almagro, J., Delgado-Rodríguez, M., Rubio-Alvarez, A., & Gómez-Salgado, J. (2019). Women's quality of life at 6 weeks postpartum: influence of the discomfort present in the puerperium. *International Journal of Environmental Research and Public Health*, *16*(2), 253.

Mastina, M., & Murdani, M. (2019). Correlation between maternal age and cesarean section. *Jurnal Kebidanan dan Keperawatan Aisyiyah*, *15*(2), 168–175.

McGrath, P., Phillips, E., & Vaughan, G. (2010). Vaginal birth after caesarean risk decision making: Australian findings on the mothers' perspective. *International Journal of Nursing Practice*, *16*(3), 274–281.

Miller, S., Abalos, E., Chamillard, M., Ciapponi, A., Colaci, D., Comandé, D., ... & Althabe, F. (2016). Beyond too little, too late and too much, too soon: a pathway towards evidence-based, respectful maternity care worldwide. *The Lancet*, *388*(10056), 2176–2192.

Mohammadi, S., Essén, B., Fallahian, M., Taheripanah, R., Saleh Gargari, S., & Källestål, C. (2016). Maternal near miss at university hospitals with cesarean overuse: an incident case control study. *Acta Obstetricia et Gynecologica Scandinavica*, *95*(7), 777–786.

Montori, M. G., Martínez, A. Á., Álvarez, C. L., Cuchí, N. A., Alcalá, P. M., & Ruiz-Martínez, S. (2021). Advanced maternal age and adverse pregnancy outcomes: a cohort study. *Taiwanese Journal of Obstetrics and Gynecology*, *60*(1), 119–124.

Moran, P. S., Normand, C., Gillen, P., Wuytack, F., Turner, M., Begley, C., & Daly, D. (2020). Economic implications of reducing caesarean section rates–analysis of two health systems. *PloS One*, *15*(7), e0228309.

Mortensen, B., Diep, L. M., Lukasse, M., Lieng, M., Dwekat, I., Elias, D., & Fosse, E. (2019). Women's satisfaction with midwife-led continuity of care: an observational study in Palestine. *BMJ Open*, *9*(11), e030324.

Mose, A., & Abebe, H. (2021). Magnitude and associated factors of caesarean section deliveries among women who gave birth in Southwest Ethiopia: institutional-based cross-sectional study. *Archives of Public Health*, *79*(1), 1–9.

Mselle, L. T., Kohi, T. W., & Dol, J. (2018). Barriers and facilitators to humanizing birth care in Tanzania: findings from semi-structured interviews with midwives and obstetricians. *Reproductive Health*, *15*(1), 1–10.

Murray, E., Pollack, L., White, M., & Lo, B. (2007). Clinical decision-making: physicians' preferences and experiences. *BMC Family Practice*, *8*(1), 10.

Mushinski, D., Zahran, S., & Frazier, A. (2021). Physician behaviour, malpractice risk and defensive medicine: an investigation of cesarean deliveries. *Health Economics, Policy and Law*, *17*(3), 247–265. 10.1017/S1744133120000432

Najmabadi, K. M., Tabatabaie, M. G., Vedadhir, A. A., & Mobarakabadi, S. S. (2020). The marginalisation of midwifery in medicalised pregnancy and childbirth: a qualitative study. *British Journal of Midwifery*, *28*(11), 768–776.

Narayan, B., & Nelson-Piercy, C. (2017). Medical problems in pregnancy. *Clinical Medicine*, *17*(3), 251.

Negrini, R., da Silva Ferreira, R. D., & Guimarães, D. Z. (2021). Value-based care in obstetrics: comparison between vaginal birth and caesarean section. *BMC Pregnancy and Childbirth*, *21*(1), 1–10.

Nyamtema, A. S., Scott, H., Kweyamba, E., Bulemela, J., Shayo, A., Mtey, G., ... & LeBlanc, J. C. (2021). Improving access, quality and safety of caesarean section services in underserved rural Tanzania: the impact of knowledge translation strategies. *African Journal of Reproductive Health*, *25*(3s), 74–83.

Nyfløt, L. T., Sandven, I., Stray-Pedersen, B., Pettersen, S., Al-Zirqi, I., Rosenberg, M., ... & Vangen, S. (2017). Risk factors for severe postpartum hemorrhage: a case-control study. *BMC Pregnancy and Childbirth*, *17*(1), 1–9.

Olaru, O. G., Stanescu, A. D., Raduta, C., Ples, L., Vasilache, A., Bacalbasa, N., ... & Balalau, O. D. (2021). Caesarean section versus vaginal birth in the perception of woman who gave birth by both methods. *Journal of Mind and Medical Sciences*, *8*(1), 127–132.

Orji, E. O., Ogunniyi, S. O., & Onwudiegwu, U. (2003). Beliefs and perceptions of pregnant women at Ileşa about caesarean section. *Tropical Journal of Obstetrics and Gynaecology*, *20*(2), 141–143.

Ormesher, L., Johnstone, E. D., Shawkat, E., Dempsey, A., Chmiel, C., Ingram, E., ... & Myers, J. E. (2018). A clinical evaluation of placental growth factor in routine practice in high-risk women presenting with suspected pre-eclampsia and/or fetal growth restriction. *Pregnancy Hypertension*, *14*, 234–239.

Otieno, D. O., & Akwala, A. (2021). Role of interpersonal communication in adoption of elective caesarean section: a study of couples in Nairobi, Kenya. In *Dialectical Perspectives on Media, Health, and Culture in Modern Africa* (pp. 75–90). IGI Global.

Pacheco-Y Orozco, F. A., Lezama-Villamil, F. G., Carrillo-Colorado, A., Amaro-García, E. J., & Dueñas-Arau, M. D. L. Á. (2021). Early vs delayed cord clamping and early skin-to-skin contact in cesarean section. *Ginecología y obstetricia de México*, *89*(6), 453–463.

Pang, M. W., Leung, T. N., Lau, T. K., & Hang Chung, T. K. (2008). Impact of first childbirth on changes in women's preference for mode of delivery: follow-up of a longitudinal observational study. *Birth*, *35*(2), 121–128.

Parikh, K. S., & Pandya, S. T. (2021). "Too powerful to push": a rise in "on demand" caesarean section. *Journal of Obstetric Anaesthesia and Critical Care*, *11*(2), 56.

Peberdy, L., Young, J., Massey, D., & Kearney, L. (2022). Integrated review of the knowledge, attitudes, and practices of maternity health care professionals concerning umbilical cord clamping. *Birth*. 1–21.

Pereira, S. L., Silva, T. P. R. D., Moreira, A. D., Novaes, T. G., Pessoa, M. C., Matozinhos, I. P., & Matozinhos, F. P. (2019). Factors associated with the length of hospital stay of women undergoing cesarean section. *Revista de Saude Publica*, *53*, 65.

Poder, T. G., & Larivière, M. (2014). Advantages and disadvantages of water birth. A systematic review of the literature. *Gynecologie, Obstetrique & Fertilite*, *42*(10), 706–771.

Purisch, S. E., Ananth, C. V., Arditi, B., Mauney, L., Ajemian, B., Heiderich, A., ... & Gyamfi-Bannerman, C. (2019). Effect of delayed vs immediate umbilical cord clamping on maternal blood loss in term cesarean delivery: a randomized clinical trial. *JAMA*, *322*(19), 1869–1876.

Quibel, T., Ghout, I., Goffinet, F., Salomon, L. J., Fort, J., Javoise, S., ... & Rozenberg, P. (2016). Active management of the third stage of labor with a combination of oxytocin and misoprostol to prevent postpartum hemorrhage. *Obstetrics & Gynecology*, *128*(4), 805–811.

Ragusa, A., Ushiro, S., Svelato, A., Strambi, N., & Tommaso, M. D. (2021). Obstetric Safety Patient. In *Textbook of Patient Safety and Clinical Risk Management* (pp. 205–212). Cham: Springer.

Rani, S., & Ayyavoo, C. (2016). Normal Puerperium. *A Practical Guide to Third Trimester of Pregnancy & Puerperium*, 28.

Ranjbar, F., Gharacheh, M., & Vedadhir, A. (2019). Overmedicalization of pregnancy and childbirth. *International Journal of Women's Health and Reproduction Sciences*, *7*, 419–420.

Rasool, M. F., Akhtar, S., Hussain, I., Majeed, A., Imran, I., Saeed, H., ... & Alqhtani, H. (2021). A cross-sectional study to assess the frequency and risk factors associated with cesarean section in Southern Punjab, Pakistan. *International Journal of Environmental Research and Public Health*, *18*(16), 8812.

Rayment-Jones, H., Dalrymple, K., Harris, J., Harden, A., Parslow, E., Georgi, T., & Sandall, J. (2021). Project20: does continuity of care and community-based antenatal care improve maternal and neonatal birth outcomes for women with social risk factors? A prospective, observational study. *PloS One*, *16*(5), e0250947.

Reyes, E., & Rosenberg, K. (2019). Maternal motives behind elective cesarean sections. *American Journal of Human Biology*, *31*(2), e23226.

Richards, M. K., Flanagan, M. R., Littman, A. J., Burke, A. K., & Callegari, L. S. (2016). Primary cesarean section and adverse delivery outcomes among women of very advanced maternal age. *Journal of Perinatology*, *36*(4), 272–277.

Robson, M., Murphy, M., & Byrne, F. (2015). Quality assurance: the 10-Group Classification System (Robson classification), induction of labor, and cesarean delivery. *International Journal of Gynecology & Obstetrics*, *131*, S23–S27.

Rocca-Ihenacho, L., & Alonso, C. (2020). Where do women birth during a pandemic? Changing perspectives on Safe Motherhood during the COVID-19 pandemic. *Journal of Global Health Science, 2*(e4), 1–9.

Roy, A., Paul, P., Chouhan, P., Rahaman, M., & Kapasia, N. (2021). Geographical variability and factors associated with caesarean section delivery in India: a comparative assessment of Bihar and Tamil Nadu. *BMC Public Health, 21*(1), 1–15.

Rudey, E. L., do Carmo Leal, M., & Rego, G. (2021). Defensive medicine and cesarean sections in Brazil. *Medicine, 100*(1).

Rydahl, E., Declercq, E., Juhl, M., & Maimburg, R. D. (2019). Cesarean section on a rise—does advanced maternal age explain the increase? A population register-based study. *PloS One, 14*(1).

Sahlin, M., Wiklund, I., Andolf, E., Löfgren, M., & Carlander, A. K. K. (2021). An Undesired Life Event": a retrospective interview study of Swedish women's experiences of Caesarean Section in the 1970s and 1980s. *Sexual & Reproductive Healthcare, 27*, 100581.

Sanavi, F. S., Rakhshani, F., Ansari-Moghaddam, A., & Edalatian, M. (2012). Reasons for elective cesarean section amongst pregnant women: a qualitative study. *Journal of Reproduction & Infertility, 13*(4), 237.

Sanchez-Ramos, L., Mantel, G. D., Moodley, J., & Burrows, R. (2001). For breech presentation at term, planned cesarean section had better neonatal outcome than planned vaginal birth. *Evidence-based Obstetrics & Gynecology, 1*(3), 5–7.

Sandall, J., Tribe, R. M., Avery, L., Mola, G., Visser, G. H., Homer, C. S., ... & Temmerman, M. (2018). Short-term and long-term effects of caesarean section on the health of women and children. *The Lancet, 392*(10155), 1349–1357.

Sanders, R. A., & Crozier, K. (2018). How do informal information sources influence women's decision-making for birth? A meta-synthesis of qualitative studies. *BMC Pregnancy and Childbirth, 18*(1), 1–26.

Schantz, C., de Loenzien, M., Goyet, S., Ravit, M., Dancoisne, A., & Dumont, A. (2019). How is women's demand for caesarean section measured? A systematic literature review. *PloS One, 14*(3), e0213352.

Schantz, C., Pantelias, A. C., de Loenzien, M., Ravit, M., Rozenberg, P., Louis-Sylvestre, C., & Goyet, S. (2021). 'A caesarean section is like you've never delivered a baby': a mixed methods study of the experience of childbirth among French women. *Reproductive Biomedicine & Society Online, 12*, 69–78.

Sentilhes, L., Merlot, B., Madar, H., Sztark, F., Brun, S., & Deneux-Tharaux, C. (2016). Postpartum haemorrhage: prevention and treatment. *Expert Review of Hematology, 9*(11), 1043–1061.

Serrano, S., & Ayres-de-Campos, D. (2021). Normal labour. *The EBCOG Postgraduate Textbook of Obstetrics & Gynaecology: Obstetrics & Maternal-Fetal Medicine, 1*, 359.

Shetty, R. K., Samant, P. Y., & Honavar, P. U. (2021). Obstetric violence: a health system study. *International Journal of Reproduction, Contraception, Obstetrics and Gynecology, 10*(4), 1551–1561.

Shirzad, M., Shakibazadeh, E., Hajimiri, K., Betran, A. P., Jahanfar, S., Bohren, M. A., ... & Abedini, M. (2021). Prevalence of and reasons for women's, family members', and health professionals' preferences for cesarean section in Iran: a mixed-methods systematic review. *Reproductive Health, 18*(1), 1–30.

Sindiani, A., Rawashdeh, H., Obeidat, N., & Zayed, F. (2020). Factors that influenced pregnant women with one previous caesarean section regarding their mode of delivery. *Annals of Medicine and Surgery, 55*, 124–130.

Smith, V., Hannon, K., & Begley, C. (2021). Clinician's attitudes towards caesarean section: a cross-sectional survey in two tertiary level maternity units in Ireland. *Women and Birth*.

Sobhy, S., Arroyo-Manzano, D., Murugesu, N., Karthikeyan, G., Kumar, V., Kaur, I., ... & Thangaratinam, S. (2019). Maternal and perinatal mortality and complications associated with caesarean section in low-income and middle-income countries: a systematic review and meta-analysis. *The Lancet, 393*(10184), 1973–1982.

Sosa, G. A., Crozier, K. E., & Stockl, A. (2018). Midwifery one-to-one support in labour: more than a ratio. *Midwifery, 62*, 230–239.

Souza, J. P., Gülmezoglu, A. M., Lumbiganon, P., Laopaiboon, M., Carroli, G., Fawole, B., & Ruyan, P. (2010). Caesarean section without medical indications is associated with an increased risk of adverse short-term maternal outcomes: the 2004–2008 WHO Global Survey on Maternal and Perinatal Health. *BMC Medicine, 8*(1), 1–10.

Spatz, D. L. (2022). Benefits of mother–baby skin-to-skin contact. *MCN: The American Journal of Maternal/Child Nursing, 47*(3), 170.

Stoll, K. H., Hauck, Y. L., Downe, S., Payne, D., & Hall, W. A. (2017). Preference for cesarean section in young nulligravid women in eight OECD countries and implications for reproductive health education. *Reproductive Health, 14*(1), 116.

Surak, A., & Elsayed, Y. (2022). Delayed cord clamping: time for physiologic implementation. *Journal of Neonatal-Perinatal Medicine*, (Preprint), 1–9.

Tadevosyan, M., Ghazaryan, A., Harutyunyan, A., Petrosyan, V., Atherly, A., & Hekimian, K. (2019). Factors contributing to rapidly increasing rates of cesarean section in Armenia: a partially mixed concurrent quantitative-qualitative equal status study. *BMC Pregnancy and Childbirth, 19*(1), 2.

Thavagnanam, S., Fleming, J., Bromley, A., Shields, M. D., & Cardwell, C. R. (2008). A meta-analysis of the association between caesarean section and childhood asthma. *Clinical & Experimental Allergy, 38*(4), 629–633.

Timofeev, J., Reddy, U. M., Huang, C. C., Driggers, R. W., Landy, H. J., & Laughon, S. K. (2013). Obstetric complications, neonatal morbidity, and indications for cesarean delivery by maternal age. *Obstetrics and Gynecology, 122*(6), 1184.

Tohid, S. Q., & St, E. N. (2011). How do women's decisions process to elective cesarean? a qualitative study. *Australian Journal of Basic and Applied Sciences, 5*(6), 210–215.

Topçu, S. (2021). Banning caesareans or selling 'Choice'?: the paradoxical regulation of caesarean section epidemics and the maternal body in Turkey. In Dayı, A., Topçu, S., & Yarar, B. (Eds.), *The Politics of the Female Body in Contemporary Turkey: Reproduction, Maternity, Sexuality* (pp. 103–126). London: I.B. Tauris. Retrieved September 18, 2022. 10.5040/9780755617432

Torkan, B., Parsay, S., Lamyian, M., Kazemnejad, A., & Montazeri, A. (2009). Postnatal quality of life in women after normal vaginal delivery and caesarean section. *BMC Pregnancy and Childbirth, 9*(1), 4.

Waldenström, U., & Ekéus, C. (2017). Risk of obstetric anal sphincter injury increases with maternal age irrespective of parity: a population-based register study. *BMC Pregnancy and Childbirth, 17*(1), 306.

Walker, K. F., & Thornton, J. G. (2021). Timing and mode of delivery with advancing maternal age. *Best Practice & Research Clinical Obstetrics & Gynaecology*, 70, 101–111.

Webb, R., Bond, R., Romero-Gonzalez, B., Mycroft, R., & Ayers, S. (2021). Interventions to treat fear of childbirth in pregnancy: a systematic review and meta-analysis. *Psychological Medicine*, 51(12), 1964–1977. 10.1017/S0033291721002324

Weeks, A. D. (2017). The puerperium. In *Obstetrics* (pp. 273–296). CRC Press.

Widström, A. M., Brimdyr, K., Svensson, K., Cadwell, K., & Nissen, E. (2019). Skin-to-skin contact the first hour after birth, underlying implications and clinical practice. *Acta Paediatrica*, 108(7), 1192–1204.

World Health Organization. (2018). *WHO recommendations on intrapartum care for a positive childbirth experience*. World Health Organization.

Zwecker, P., Azoulay, L., & Abenhaim, H. A. (2011). Effect of fear of litigation on obstetric care: a nationwide analysis on obstetric practice. *American Journal of Perinatology*, 28(04), 277–284.

4 Italian experience in the international context: empirical evidence from two case studies

Gabriella Piscopo and Margherita Ruberto

4.1 Introduction to case studies

The dramatic increase in the practice of cesarean section has raised interest in understanding the factors that influence the decision to use this procedure, which, over the years, has lost its emergency meaning, becoming a type of choice conditioned less by the presence of real medical risk factors than by a number of different factors that lead to increasingly inappropriate decisions from a clinical and organizational point of view. Understanding and addressing these motivations is precisely the key to reducing inappropriate use of this practice (Bailit, 2012; Boerma et al., 2018; Can et al., 2016; Dweik et al., 2014; Elnakib et al., 2019; Ji et al., 2015; Mylonas & Friese, 2015; Toker et al., 2019).

Through the analysis of factors of variation in cesarean section rates, this research aims at supporting the formulation of appropriate clinical and managerial decisions with respect to the most suitable mode of childbirth and at promoting an informed and rational use of the practice of cesarean section.

On the basis of data and information obtained from the main sources of information relating to the birth event, a dataset was constructed in which clinical and extra-clinical variables that correlate with the mode of childbirth were reported in order to carry out a descriptive study on the multidimensional nature of the phenomenon. The project activity included a cognitive survey of the organizational and procedural aspects applied to the two Italian hospitals in southern Italy under investigation.

The research questions for the study were as follows:

- RQ1: Is there an association between mode of delivery and mode of labor?
- RQ2: Is there an association between mode of delivery and occupational status?
- RQ3: Is there an association between mode of delivery and maternal age?
- RQ4: Is there an association between mode of delivery and educational qualification?

DOI: 10.4324/9781003330097-5

- RQ5: Is there an association between mode of delivery and previous conceptions?

4.1.1 The Italian context

Each pregnancy and delivery narrative has a unique course with a range of clinical, administrative, and emotional characteristics. However, it is the responsibility of the general public to make the journey as easy as possible by removing stressors, providing information, developing new parents' skills, easing anxiety, promoting the continuation of compassionate and humane support even after leaving medical facilities, and striking a balance between the requirements and standards of clinical safety and the understanding that, except in rare circumstances, childbirth is a natural phenomenon and not a disease. Some distinctively Italian flaws may be seen in this overall picture, which European and national data neglect to mention: a lack of functional territorial medicine, which leads to a forced and heavy entry of pregnancies into outpatient and hospital procedures, sometimes without real need; a significant fragmentation of the network of birth points, often at the expense of care quality; an overreliance on surgical delivery; Italian women's concern with motherhood, primarily as a result of the lack of support services for children's early development; and inadequate preparation to cope with the increased number of foreign women in the country, who are often not even able to understand the Italian language.

At the conclusion of the first decade of the 2000s, a number of recommendations and guidance tools aimed at health workers, administrators, and families were produced with the intention of making the birth route safer while also "humanizing" it. In particular, at the end of 2010, a system of guidelines related to physiological pregnancy and the reduction of cesarean deliveries was drafted and disseminated, outlining an ideal pregnancy pathway in terms of both territorial planning and improving the modalities of care and treatment, to encourage the dissemination of information to prepare, support, and reassure women. Among the ten points of the agreement, some are particularly indicative of what might be called an ideal model of the pathway in light of four main objectives:

- to humanize the journey by minimizing the use of medicine while enhancing elements like information, easing pain and stress, and assisting new parents in taking care of the infant, with a focus on teaching breastfeeding to mothers in particular;
- to make diagnostic and therapeutic operations, as well as delivery, safe by safeguarding birth sites, making care facilities more efficient, and enhancing emergency response capabilities;
- to encourage integration and continuity of treatment between the hospital and the community, with a focus on bolstering the network of

family counseling centers and social services for handling the most delicate circumstances;
- to close the gap between the north-central and southern areas to begin reducing territorial imbalances.

In partnership with 60 Healthcare Centers in 15 regions and autonomous provinces, the Istituto Superiore di Sanità conducted a study in 2022 that examined how individuals are born in Italy today. The poll was designed to characterize the many stages of the event, from pregnancy through the child's first year of life, and was based on a sample of 7640 women in the year following childbirth. The effect of information and counseling provided to the mother on the decisions she made during pregnancy, delivery, and the months that followed the birth was one of the study's most important results. The results reveal a very unbalanced scenario, with certain regions, particularly in the south, seeing childbirth as a period of significant medicalization and others where knowledge encourages natural birthing and early and prolonged nursing.

Only 30% of women attend birthing education classes, and 75% of women have private gynecologists monitor them during their pregnancies. Geographical location and educational attainment seem to play a role in this decision, with less educated women, housewives, and southern areas being not particularly involved. Additionally, there is evidence that people tend to get more ultrasounds (4 to 7 on average) than the three the Ministry of Health advised.

Regional differences in the amount of information received from healthcare professionals about birthing are obvious. Even though the Ministry of Health has made a particular recommendation in this respect since the mid-1980s, there is still very little information provided to women after childbirth on the postpartum course and the resumption of sexual activity. In Italy, for example, the prevalence of cesarean deliveries has significantly grown over the previous 20 years, rising from 11.2% in 1980 to 33.2% in 2000. This number is significantly higher than in other European nations (e.g., 21.5% in England and Wales, 17.8% in Spain, and 15.9% in France), as well as 10–15% higher than recommended by the World Health Organization. There is also a substantial amount of geographical variation, with a low in the north of Italy of 18.7% and a high in the south of Italy, notably in the Campania area, of 53.4% in 2000. In southern Italy, the biggest increases were noted (from 8.5% in 1980 to 53.4% in 2000 in Campania region). Private clinics recorded higher rates of cesarean section utilization and greater yearly increases.

4.1.2 Theoretical foundation: the T.R.E.E. model

This study is part of a research project created under the auspices of the DAOSan Master's (Management of Healthcare Companies and Organizations)

Program and the Interdepartmental Center for Research in Law, Economics and Management of Public Administration (CIRPA) of the University of Salerno in Italy. This project, called "T.R.E.E. – Targeted exploration, Reconfiguration, Evaluation, and Exhibition," aims to activate paths of mutual fertilization between theory and practice in order to promote cultural and business developments in a perspective of continuous improvement of the quality of services rendered to citizens and efficiency in the use of public resources (Adinolfi & Giancotti, 2021).

Pursuing an ideal balance between different possible approaches to change (top-down, outside-in and inside-up), the project aimed to combine the commitment of institutional stakeholders and the contribution of external consultants to the "bottom-up movement," in which learners actively collaborate with partner companies in a process of learning-experimentation in the field.

The tree is an effective metaphor. Each learner, as well as each project, can be seen as a tree (Adinolfi & Giancotti, 2021): at first it is a sprout; then, gradually, it grows and develops a trunk, from which the various branches develop and evolve, producing leaves and fruit. Each branch represents a direction following a choice. The tree lives because it is rooted in soil (i.e., the substrate of cultural values nurtured through the formative path). Its energy starts from deep, hidden roots, which allow the tree to bear fruit by sinking into the vast soil from which it draws nourishment. Moreover, nourishment can also come from interaction with the external environment. Fruits represent the coagulation of energy flowing through the tree, allowing the seed to be cast into the soil to give birth to a new cycle. Leaves and fruits, as they fall to the ground, help produce nourishment that is absorbed by the roots. They are returned to the soil below the tree as well as to the neighboring soil.

T.R.E.E. is thus a model intended to empower the actors of the training course to identify innovative ways to produce value, design the best possible organization (with the best combination of resources), and evaluate and communicate its impact in terms of costs, risks, and outcomes.

In the three-year period of 2014–2017, the model was applied to a group of southern healthcare and hospital companies, involving Master's students in an analysis of cost determinants of healthcare performance and a study of organizational processes with the aims of:

- producing innovation in terms of rationalization and qualification of health services;
- applying, according to an innovative and harmonized approach, the tools of organizational analysis and cost measurement to a group of healthcare organizations active in Southern Italy;
- establishing a task force of professionals from within the healthcare organizations, equipped with homogeneous skills and tools, to promote change in the local healthcare system in a coordinated and incisive manner.

In a relentless effort to recontextualize and recalibrate the training course on new emerging issues, since 2018 the focus has shifted to the themes of management and organizational and digital innovation in healthcare companies.

Partly thanks to the impetus of the DAOSan Steering Committee, the Master's program has been the promoter of a Technical Table with representatives of institutions and administrators of public and private companies in the healthcare and allied sectors, aimed at discussing strategies for improving healthcare services, from which emerged a huge need for innovation and a strong need for distinctive skills in the implementation of innovative projects in healthcare.

4.1.3 Data collection

To create a model to redesign the birth path, a comparison was made between the organizational models of the birth path adopted by two hospital facilities in the Campania region of Southern Italy. These facilities perform more than 1,000 deliveries per year, most of which are spontaneous deliveries (Table 4.1).

First, a retrospective observational design was adopted to explore the characteristics of the selected sample and achieve the objective of controlling the risk of clinically unnecessary cesarean section.

The project activity included a survey of the organizational and procedural aspects applied at the units under investigation (i.e., the Department of Gynecology and Obstetrics of both hospitals). The sample under analysis included women who gave birth in the year 2018. The mode of the requested data was anonymous for scientific research purposes. That is, the data were processed using techniques that do not allow the identity of the subject to be traced and which, therefore, lose the characteristic of "personal data." As such, the processing of the data does not require specific and further consent of the interested parties.

The first phase of the study was dedicated to the consultation of the main sources of information related to the birth event: Certificates of Birth Assistance (CeDAPs) and Hospital Discharge Cards (SDOs). In particular, the CeDAPs are the richest source of health, epidemiological,

Table 4.1 Sample characteristics

Hospital	No. of total deliveries	No. of spontaneous deliveries	% of spontaneous deliveries	No. of cesarean sections	% of cesarean sections
1	1823	813	44.6	1010	55.4
2	1136	755	66.5	381	34.5

and socio-demographic information on the event of birth, while the SDOs are administrative tools for collecting information on each patient discharged from public and private hospitals throughout the country.

From the CeDAPs, it is possible to obtain a series of information such as:

- data related to the structure in which the event takes place;
- maternal socio-demographic data: name, surname, tax code, date of birth, municipality of birth, citizenship status, municipality of residence, region of residence, ASL of residence, educational qualification, professional status, and marital status; information on the medical conditions of the mother during pregnancy: degree of consanguinity between mother and father, previous conceptions (number of deliveries, live births, stillbirths, miscarriages, IVGs, and cesareans), date of last delivery, mother's height, pre-pregnancy weight, mother's weight at delivery, date of last menstruation, gestational age, mother's blood group, Rh prophylaxis;
- information related to services used in pregnancy, checkups in pregnancy (number of checkups in pregnancy, number of ultrasounds, time of the first visit), attendance of the pre-birth course, course and care of pregnancy, conception with assisted reproduction technique, smoking habits in the 5 years preceding pregnancy;
- information related to prenatal investigations: chorionic villus sampling, translucency, bitest, amniocentesis, fetoscopy/funiculocentesis, structural morphological ultrasound, ultrasound performed after 22 weeks, anti-rubella Ig antibody test, anti-toxoplasmosis Ig antibody test, anti-CMV IgG antibody test, anti-HbsAg antibody test;
- information related to labor and delivery: place of delivery, date of delivery, municipality where delivery occurred, mode of labor, type and reason for induction, gender of delivery (no. of male births, no. of female births), health personnel present at the time of delivery, episiotomy performed.

The SDOs form an integral part of the medical record and, in addition to containing personal data and information about the facility where the hospitalization took place, enrich the CEDAP with clinical information (main and secondary diagnoses, diagnostic procedures, major and minor interventions, admission and discharge information) that allows for a more in-depth study of the medicalization of the pregnancy-partum pathway.

Hospital discharge data were collected using the DRGs (Diagnosis Related Groups) methodology, an iso-resource classification system that allows all discharged patients to be divided into categories called MDCs (Major Diagnostic Categories). In particular, DRGs 370–375 were consulted:

- DRG 370 (delivery by cesarean section with complications) and DRG 371 (delivery by cesarean section without complications) were used to identify cesarean sections.

- DRG 372 (vaginal delivery with complicating diagnoses), DRG 373 (vaginal delivery without complicating diagnoses), DRG 374 (vaginal delivery with sterilization and/or dilation and curettage), and DRG 375 (vaginal delivery with other intervention except sterilization and/or dilation and curettage) were used to identify vaginal deliveries.

Based on evidence from the scientific literature as well as data and information obtained from CeDAPs and SDOs, a dataset was constructed through which to identify the associations between the factors that determine the higher probability of recourse to cesarean section (Tables 4.2 and 4.3).

4.1.4 Data analysis

The analyzed dataset presents 433 observations and 50 variables. Descriptive statistics were analyzed for the variables examined, with frequency tables for qualitative variables and position and variability indices for quantitative

Table 4.2 Hospital 1's DRG, weight, threshold, and ordinary admissions

Hospital 1					
DRG	Weight	Threshold	Ordinary admissions (duration 0–1 day) (in Euros)	Ordinary admissions (duration >1 day) (in Euros)	Day over threshold (in Euros)
370	0.964	14		2.503,80	153,00
371	0.733	6		1.882,80	153,00
372	0.565	8	199,80	1.457,10	135,00
373	0.444	5	199,80	1.144,80	133,20
374	0.695	8	573,30	1.909,80	157,50
375	0.914	8		2.573,10	171,00

Table 4.3 Hospital 2's DRG, weight, threshold, and ordinary admissions

Hospital 2					
DRG	Weight	Threshold	Ordinary admissions (duration 0–1 day) (in Euros)	Ordinary admissions (duration >1 day) (in Euros)	Day over threshold (in Euros)
370	0.964	14		2.782,00	170,00
371	0.733	6		2.092,00	170,00
372	0.565	8	222,00	1.619,00	150,00
373	0.444	5	222,00	1.272,00	148,00
374	0.695	8	637,00	2.122,00	174,00
375	0.914	8		2.859,00	190,00

variables. Statistical tests were then performed to assess whether there was any statistical correlation or difference in the averages between the variables, in relation to the type of delivery: the Chi-test was performed for the qualitative variables, while the independent samples t-test was performed for the quantitative variables. Finally, a logistic regression was performed to highlight possible predictors for the dependent variable "type of delivery." The software used for the analysis was SPSS version 25.

4.1.4.1 Chi-square test – mode of delivery and mode of labor

We proceeded to perform a chi-square test between the variable "mode of delivery" and the variable "mode of labor." We proceeded by first analyzing the contingency tables (Tables 4.4 and 4.5).

Since the test was statistically significant, Cramer's V was interpreted. This value defines the "strength of the association" and can be interpreted as follows:

- if the V is between 0 and 0.33, the association is of slight intensity;
- if the V is between 0.33 and 0.66, the association is of moderate intensity;
- if the V is between 0.66 and 1, the association is of strong intensity.

In this case, Cramer's V equal to 0.721 shows that this association is of strong intensity.

Table 4.4 Mode of delivery and mode of labor contingency table

		Mode of labor				
		Without labor (for elective CT only)	Labor with spontaneous onset	Piloted spontaneous onset labor	Induced labor	Total
Mode of delivery	Natural childbirth	0	172	1	16	189
	Cesarean section	176	56	1	11	244
Total		176	228	2	27	433

Table 4.5 Mode of delivery and mode of labor chi-square test

	Value	gl	Asymptotic significance (bilateral)
Pearson chi-square	225,167	3	,000
Likelihood ratio	278,986	3	,000
Linear by linear association	113,523	1	,000
No. of valid cases	433		

Italian experience in the international context 77

4.1.4.2 Chi-square test – mode of delivery and professional condition

In this case, a chi-square test has been conducted between the variable "mode of delivery" and the variable "professional condition" (Tables 4.6 and 4.7).

4.1.4.3 Chi-square test – mode of delivery and maternal age

A chi-square test has been conducted between the variable "mode of delivery" and the variable "maternal age" (Tables 4.8 and 4.9).

4.1.4.4 Chi-square test – mode of delivery and title of study

A chi-square test has been conducted between the variable "mode of delivery" and the variable "title of study" (Tables 4.10 and 4.11).

Table 4.6 Mode of delivery and professional condition contingency table

		\multicolumn{4}{c}{*Professional condition*}
		Housewife	*Unemployed/ student*	*Employed*	*Total*
Mode of delivery	**Natural childbirth**	59	39	91	189
	Cesarean section	67	57	120	244
Total		126	96	211	433

Table 4.7 Mode of delivery and professional condition chi-square test

	Value	*gl*	*Asymptotic significance (bilateral)*
Pearson chi-square	,897	2	,639
Likelihood ratio	,897	2	,639
Linear by linear association	,330	1	,566
No. of valid cases	433		

Table 4.8 Mode of delivery and maternal age contingency table

		\multicolumn{4}{c}{*Maternal age (in years)*}
		<18–24	*25–34*	*35->45*	*Total*
Mode of delivery	**Natural childbirth**	15	103	71	189
	Cesarean section	21	128	95	244
Total		36	231	166	433

Table 4.9 Mode of delivery and maternal age chi-square test

	Value	gl	Asymptotic significance (bilateral)
Pearson chi-square	,192	2	,908
Likelihood ratio	,193	2	,908
Linear by linear association	,014	1	,907
No. of valid cases	433		

Table 4.10 Mode of delivery and title of study contingency table

		Title of study			
		Elementary/ middle school	High school diploma	Degree	Total
Mode of delivery	Natural childbirth	37	86	65	188
	Cesarean section	54	111	76	241
Total		91	197	141	429

Table 4.11 Mode of delivery and title of study chi-square test

	Value	gl	Asymptotic significance (bilateral)
Pearson chi-square	,669	2	,716
Likelihood ratio	,670	2	,715
Linear by linear association	,664	1	,415
No. of valid cases	429		

4.1.4.5 Chi-square test – mode of delivery and previous conceptions

A chi-square test has been conducted between the variable "mode of delivery" and the the variable "previous conceptions" (Tables 4.12 and 4.13).

4.1.4.6 Independent-samples t-test of mode of delivery and number of cesareans

An independent-samples t-test was performed to test whether there is a statistically significant difference in the mean of the "number of cesareans" variable in the two subgroups of the "mode of delivery" variable. The null hypothesis of the independent samples t-test is that the averages are equal in the two groups, while the alternative hypothesis is that the averages differ significantly in population. We will reject the null hypothesis of equal averages, concluding that the averages are significantly different, if the p-value turns out to be less than 0.05.

Table 4.12 Mode of delivery and previous conceptions contingency table

		Previous conceptions		
		Yes	No	Total
Mode of delivery	Natural childbirth	101	88	189
	Cesarean section	96	148	244
Total		197	236	433

Prior to the t-test, Levene's test is performed to verify the null hypothesis of equal variances in the two subgroups. If this assumption is violated ($p < 0.05$), the robust t-test is performed; that is, the results are reported in the second line of the output. The mean of the variable "number of cesareans" appears to be lower in natural childbirth than in cesarean delivery; however, to determine whether or not this difference is statistically significant, we need to perform the independent sample test (Tables 4.14 and 4.15).

Levene's test rejects the null hypothesis of equal variances ($p < 0.001$), so the robust t-test (second row) is performed. The robust t-test rejects the null hypothesis of equal means ($p < 0.001$).

It is concluded, therefore, that the mean of the variable "number of cesareans" is significantly different in the two groups, and, in particular, the mean of the subgroup "natural childbirth" is significantly lower (by 0.480) than the mean of the subgroup "cesarean section."

4.1.4.7 Logistic regression

We proceed with the implementation of logistic regression.

The mode of delivery (dichotomous) was chosen as the independent variable, while educational qualification (recoded), mother's age (recoded),

Table 4.13 Mode of delivery and previous conceptions chi-square test

	Value	gl	Asymptotic significance (bilateral)
Pearson chi-square	8,570	2	,014
Likelihood ratio	8,584	2	,014
Linear by linear association	7,958	1	,005
No. of valid cases	433		

Table 4.14 Group statistics: mode of delivery and number of cesarean sections

Mode of delivery	No.	Average	Standard deviation	Average standard error
Natural childbirth	189	,05	,287	,021
Cesarean section	244	,53	,597	,038

Table 4.15 Independent-samples test

	Levene's test for the equality of variances		T-test for equality of means				
	F	Sign.	T	gl	Sign.	Difference of the mean	Standard error difference	Confidence interval of 95% difference
Assumed equal variances	329,188	,000	-10,170	431	,000	-,480	,047	-,573 -,387
Not assumed equal variances			11,014	367,139	,000	-,480	,044	-,566 -,394

participation in a pre-birth course (dichotomous), occupational status (re-coded), services used in pregnancy (recoded), and course during pregnancy were selected as the independent variables.

Only subjects without missing values (i.e., 426 subjects out of a total of 433), could be used for logistic regression.

Regarding the dependent variable, we set as mode 1 = cesarean delivery and 0 = natural delivery, and we will then interpret the results in terms of choice of type of delivery.

To choose the significant variables, a Stepwise forward methodology (Wald) was applied: that is, all the variables with p-values lower than 0.10 in the Wald test were entered.

Nagelkerke's R-square index indicates that the final model was able to explain about 1.7% of the overall variability of the phenomenon.

The specificity is equal to 23%, while the sensitivity is equal to 85.8%, indicating that the model has a good ability to correctly predict who chooses a cesarean section among all those who actually had a cesarean section, but it has a lower ability to correctly predict who will have a natural birth among those who actually have had a natural birth.

We proceed to interpret the significance and Odds Ratios of the included independent variables:

- The variable participation in the pre-birth course turns out to be statistically significant (p = 0.021). In this case, observing the Odds Ratio equal to 1.800, it can be concluded that when a woman does not participate in the pre-birth course, the probability of choosing a cesarean section over natural childbirth increases by 80%;
- The remaining variables, on the other hand, are not statistically significant, as is evident from the following table.

4.2 Results

The results of the study showed that many of the causes related to the increase in rates of cesarean section identified in the literature were found in the context under investigation. Specifically, when analyzing data from women who gave birth at the Hospital no. 2, it was found that 56.4% of women had a cesarean section delivery while 43.6% gave birth naturally.

Research question 1 explored the association between the variable "mode of delivery" and the variable "mode of labor." From the analysis conducted, it can be stated that there is a statistically significant association between the type of delivery and the mode of labor. Specifically, among natural childbirth, 94.7% had spontaneous onset labor, 0.5% had piloted spontaneous onset labor, and 8.5% had induced labor. Among those who delivered by cesarean section, 72.1% had a cesarean section by choice, 23% had spontaneous onset labor, 0.4% had piloted spontaneous onset labor, and 4.5% had induced labor.

Research question 2 examined the association between the variable "mode of delivery" and the variable "occupational status." The chi-square test was found to be statistically non-significant (p = 0.639); therefore, the null hypothesis of independence between the variables was accepted, and it was concluded that the two variables were not significantly associated. In particular, it emerged that among those who performed natural childbirth, 31.2% were housewives, 20.6% were unemployed/students, and 48.1% were employed; similarly, among those who performed cesarean section childbirth: 31.2% were housewives, 20.8% were unemployed/students, and 48.1% were employed.

Research question 3 examined the association between the variable "mode of delivery" and the variable "maternal age." It was found that among women who performed natural childbirth, 7.9% belonged to the <18–24 age group, 54.5% to the 25–34 age group, and 37.6% to the 35–45+ age group; meanwhile, among cesarean sections: 8.6% belonged to the <18–24 age group, 52.5% to the 25–34 age group, and 38.9% to the 35–45+ age group. Also, in this case, the chi-square test was statistically non-significant (p=0.908); thus, the null hypothesis of independence between the variables was accepted, and it was concluded that the two variables are not significantly associated.

Research question 4 analyzed the association between the variable "mode of delivery" and the variable "educational qualification." Among women who had a natural childbirth, 19.7% graduated from elementary or middle school, 45.7% had a high school diploma, and 34.6% had a bachelor's degree. Among those who had a delivery by cesarean section, 22% graduated from elementary or middle school, 46.1% had a high school diploma, and 31.5% had a college degree. In this case, the chi-square test was statistically non-significant (p = 0.713); therefore, we accept the null hypothesis of independence between the variables and state that the two variables are not significantly associated.

Finally, the analysis conducted showed that there was a statistically significant association between the variable "mode of delivery" and the variable "previous conceptions" (research question 5). Among those who performed natural childbirth, 53.4% had no previous conceptions, while 45.6 did have previous conceptions. Among those who had a delivery by cesarean section: 60.6% had previous conceptions, while 39.3% did not. In this case, Cramer's V, equal to 0.141, shows us that this association is of mild intensity.

Finally, the only statistically significant variable in the logistic regression model is participation in the pre-birth course, which increases the probability of choosing a cesarean section by 80% compared to natural childbirth.

4.3 Discussion

As stated earlier, this research aimed at promoting the informed use of the practice of cesarean section to support the formulation of appropriate clinical and managerial decisions and the effective implementation of the patient empowerment process. To this end, the study proposes an analysis of the factors with the greatest impact on the increase in cesarean section rates.

The results of the study conducted in Southern Italy, in facilities where a high percentage of cesarean rates have been recorded in recent years, showed that many nonclinical variables influence the choice of delivery mode. The study confirmed the association between the type of delivery and labor mode; in particular, it found that most of the cesarean sections performed were planned. This result is in line with some studies in the literature (Grant, 2005; Gruber et al., 1999; Liu et al., 2014), according to which a programmable cesarean section allows physicians to manage their professional activities and provides higher revenues to hospitals, because the reimbursement per DRG of cesarean section is higher than the reimbursement with natural childbirth. To this extent, since no clinical risk factors were found in the selected sample to justify such a high rate of cesarean sections, the main hypothesis is that the difference in rates between the two modes of delivery influences the physician's decisions, leading him or her to prefer cesarean section as a more profitable mode of delivery.

Another critical issue is the heavy reliance on private care by the sample analyzed, an aspect that strongly affects the increase in the cesarean section rate. Although the Italian public health system guarantees free maternal care to all women, most women prefer to be supported by a private gynecologist during pregnancy. In fact, the results of the analysis showed that most women were followed throughout their pregnancy by a private gynecologist. The presence of a highly personalized pregnant woman-gynecologist relationship pushes the gynecologist to necessarily have to attend the delivery of his or her patient and decreases the pregnant woman's concern about giving birth in an unfamiliar environment. The creation of this "alliance" between the pregnant woman and her trusted physician often leads to misinformation related to the misconception that cesarean delivery is safer than natural childbirth (Leeman & Rogers, 2012).

The study also found that most women who had a cesarean section in previous pregnancies underwent a cesarean section in the next pregnancy. In agreement with several studies in the literature, repeated cesarean section contributes significantly to the overall increase in cesarean section rates (Birara & Gebrehiwot, 2013; Lundgren et al., 2015; Li et al., 2019). Also, through the analysis of the SDO, it was found that the most relevant main diagnosis is "previous cesarean section" (26.8%), indicating that a woman who has previously given birth via cesarean section is undergoing a new elective cesarean section. In such a case, it is not known whether the indication of the previous cesarean is appropriate, which, however, exposes the woman, almost systematically, to the new procedure, or whether a trial delivery was done as the widespread evidence in the literature recommends

(Cunningham et al., 2011; Zhang et al., 2020). Vaginal delivery after cesarean section (VBAC) can be seen as a viable option for many women who have previously given birth via cesarean section; in fact, it is associated with several potential health benefits for women, including less medicalization and a shorter hospitalization period.

In addition, attendance at the pre-natal course was found to be very low. This is noteworthy because participation in a birth coaching course can significantly influence the mode of delivery (Cai et al., 2021). In fact, the analysis showed that nonparticipation in a pre-birth course increases the probability of choosing a cesarean delivery by 80% compared to natural delivery.

Finally, analyzing the organizational model adopted by the two hospitals, it was also found that there is a shortage of staff among midwives who are supposed to maintain a 1:1 ratio with women (Alba et al., 2019). The advantage of being followed by a midwife is related to receiving more information and greater empowerment so as to ensure the safety and physiology of the birth event (Attanasio et al., 2021; Bradfield et al., 2019; Edmons et al., 2020).

In conclusion, the results exclude, with reference to cesarean sections, an approach that is exclusively clinical; instead, they indicate a need for an organizational and multi-level analysis, which may represent a deeper paradigm shift for the topic under study. The following chapter attempts to discern these issues with the proposal of a model that also takes into consideration other aspects, such as parenthood, that are fundamental to the birth pathway.

References

Adinolfi, P., & Giancotti, F. (2021). Pedagogical triage and emergent strategies: a management educational program in pandemic times. *Sustainability*, *13*(6), 3519.

Alba, R., Franco, R., Patrizia, B., Maria, C. B., Giovanna, A., Chiara, F., & Isabella, N. (2019). The midwifery-led care model: a continuity of care model in the birth path. *Acta Bio Medica: Atenei Parmensis*, *90*(Suppl 6), 41.

Attanasio, L. B., DaCosta, M., Kleppel, R., Govantes, T., Sankey, H. Z., & Goff, S. L. (2021). Community perspectives on the creation of a hospital-based Doula program. *Health Equity*, *5*(1), 545–553.

Bailit, J. (2012). Impact of non-clinical factors on primary cesarean deliveries. *Semin Perinatol*, *36*, 395–398.

Birara, M., & Gebrehiwot, Y. (2013). Factors associated with success of vaginal birth after one caesarean section (VBAC) at three teaching hospitals in Addis Ababa, Ethiopia: a case control study. *BMC Pregnancy and Childbirth*, *13*(1), 1–6.

Boerma, T., Ronsmans, C., Melesse, D. Y., Barros, A. J., Barros, F. C., Juan, L., ... & Neto, D. D. L. R. (2018). Global epidemiology of use of and disparities in caesarean sections. *The Lancet*, *392*(10155), 1341–1348.

Bradfield, Z., Hauck, Y., Kelly, M., & Duggan, R. (2019). "It's what midwifery is all about": Western Australian midwives' experiences of being 'with woman'during labour and birth in the known midwife model. *BMC Pregnancy and Childbirth*, *19*(1), 1–13.

Cai, J., Tang, M., Gao, Y., Zhang, H., Yang, Y., Zhang, D., ... & Wu, B. (2021). Cesarean section or vaginal delivery to prevent possible vertical transmission from a pregnant mother confirmed with COVID-19 to a neonate: a systematic review. *Frontiers in Medicine*, *8*, 634949.

Can, O. N. E. R., Catak, B., Sütlü, S., & Kilinc, S. (2016). Effect of social factors on cesarean birth in Primiparous women: a cross sectional study (social factors and cesarean birth). *Iranian Journal of Public Health*, *45*(6), 768.

Cunningham, F. G., Bangdiwala, S. I., Brown, S. S., Dean, T. M., Frederiksen, M., Hogue, C. R., ... & Zimmet, S. C. (2011). National Institutes of Health consensus development conference statement: vaginal birth after cesarean section: new insights march 8–10, 2010. *Obstetric Anesthesia Digest*, *31*(3), 140–142.

Dweik, D., Girasek, E., Mészáros, G., Töreki, A., Keresztúri, A., & Pál, A. (2014). Non-medical determinants of cesarean section in a medically dominated maternity system. *Acta Obstetricia et Gynecologica Scandinavica*, *93*(10), 1025–1033.

Edmonds, J. K., Ivanof, J., & Kafulafula, U. (2020). Midwife led units: transforming maternity care globally. *Annals of Global Health*, *86*(1).

Elnakib, S., Abdel-Tawab, N., Orbay, D., & Hassanein, N. (2019). Medical and non-medical reasons for cesarean section delivery in Egypt: a hospital-based retrospective study. *BMC Pregnancy and Childbirth*, *19*(1), 1–11.

Grant, D. (2005). Explaining source of payment differences in US cesarean rates: why do privately insured mothers receive more cesareans than mothers who are not privately insured? *Health Care Management Science*, *8*(1), 5–17.

Gruber, J., Kim, J., & Mayzlin, D. (1999). Physician fees and procedure intensity: the case of cesarean delivery. *Journal of Health Economics*, *18*(4), 473–490.

Ji, H., Jiang, H., Yang, L., Qian, X., & Tang, S. (2015). Factors contributing to the rapid rise of caesarean section: a prospective study of primiparous Chinese women in Shanghai. *BMJ Open*, *5*(11), e008994.

Leeman, L. M., & Rogers, R. G. (2012). Sex after childbirth: postpartum sexual function. *Obstetrics & Gynecology*, *119*(3), 647–655.

Li, Y., Zhang, C., & Zhang, D. (2019). Cesarean section and the risk of neonatal respiratory distress syndrome: a meta-analysis. *Archives of Gynecology and Obstetrics*, *300*(3), 503–517.

Liu, Y., Li, G., Chen, Y., Wang, X., Ruan, Y., Zou, L., & Zhang, W. (2014). A descriptive analysis of the indications for caesarean section in mainland China. *BMC Pregnancy and Childbirth*, *14*(1), 1–9.

Lundgren, I., Smith, V., Nilsson, C., Vehvilainen-Julkunen, K., Nicoletti, J., Devane, D., ... & Begley, C. (2015). Clinician-centred interventions to increase vaginal birth after caesarean section (VBAC): a systematic review. *BMC Pregnancy and Childbirth*, *15*(1), 1–9.

Mylonas, I., & Friese, K. (2015). Indications for and risks of elective cesarean section. *Deutsches Ärzteblatt International*, *112*(29–30), 489.

Toker, E., Turan, Z., Omaç Sönmez, M., & Kabalcioğlu Bucak, F. (2019). Why have the numbers of cesareans increased globally? The factors that affect women's decisions about cesarean delivery in Turkey. *The Journal of Maternal-Fetal & Neonatal Medicine*, *33*(20), 3529–3537. 10.1080/14767058.2019.1644311

Zhang, J., Zhang, Y., Ma, Y., Ke, Y., Huo, S., He, L., ... & Zhao, A. (2020). The associated factors of cesarean section during COVID-19 pandemic: a cross-sectional study in nine cities of China. *Environmental Health and Preventive Medicine*, *25*(1), 1–7.

5 Towards a new model for the birth path

Gabriella Piscopo

5.1 Redesigning the birth path: towards a new model

This chapter proposes a model for redesigtning the birth path that is the result of a multidisciplinary, managerial, and clinical vision, acting on a triple level: cultural, organizational, and technological.

First, a new bio-psycho-social-cultural paradigm underlying the childbirth event is envisioned, which sees a renewed centrality of the couple and family from a fatherhood perspective.

Second, the birth path is redesigned, in organizational terms, as a Value Constellation called upon to orchestrate the value generated by the actors in the System map.

Finally, possible technological accelerators are identified, as agents at the individual and organizational level capable of governing the complex and multidimensional dimensions of the childbirth event.

The proposed model can be represented graphically as in Figure 5.1.

Viewing the birth path from a process perspective, especially when faced with the COVID-19 pandemic, stimulates reflections on the organizational and management level that lay the foundations for a New Public Governance of the childbirth event. The current healthcare context moves in a fluid and magmatic background generated by the profound process of deconstruction that the healthcare emergency induced (OASI report, 2021). The traditional organizational, structural, and disciplinary barriers typical of healthcare organizations acting as professional bureaucracies have been suddenly broken down to face the common enemy and to experiment with organizational models and settings of care that the literature and scientific evidences have not had time to validate in advance. With reference to the birth path, this radical phase of healthcare deconstruction sees in the endemic management of COVID-19 a cultural and social humus conducive to a possible business process reengineering (BPR), which starts from a primary rethinking of the underlying social and healthcare paradigm. This paradigm subsequently impacts the design of services and relationships present within the organizational ecosystem.

DOI: 10.4324/9781003330097-6

88 Gabriella Piscopo

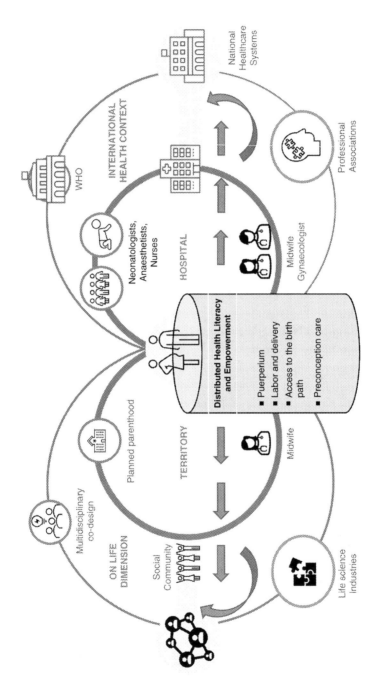

Figure 5.1 A Value Constellation for the birth path.
Source: (authors' elaboration).

Childbirth is framed as a physiological event to be "accompanied" along a care continuum of social and health services. However, management practice and scientific evidences highlight how, although the flow of the birth path is sharp and linear, within in there are pockets of unpredictability of action (e.g., improper risk stratification, predominance of private care in pregnancy, and lack of homogeneity in terms of approaches to birth management and skills for healthcare providers) and complexity related, in the main, to organizational and cultural factors. It is precisely in such multidimensional interstices of the pathway that a reductionist perspective of health risks still prevails, allowing the medical dimension of childbirth to prevail at the expense of the physiological one. These risks generate a phenomenon of value destruction (Alford, 2016; Cui & Osborne, 2022; Keeling et al., 2021) that looks at birth not as a "pathway to be accompanied" but as a set of procedures to be adhered to in a standardized approach to care.

This chapter will contain an analysis conducted in the Italian context, although limited to one regional context and therefore weakly generalizable, that returns a highly fragmented picture of the birth path. The supply of services is heterogeneous on the organizational level by virtue of the different sizes, the public or private profile of the facility, the different operational modes of childbirth care, the very modes of access to services, and the different sensitivity with respect to the centrality of the patient.

The pathway, therefore, despite being clearly designed by the guidelines promoted by institutional and scientific governance supra-systems, is strongly influenced by intra-organizational and inter-organizational determinants as well as the strong impact of extra-clinical variables.

The primary stimulus for a new model of the birth path starts from the rethinking of the patient, who is no longer identified as the woman alone, but as the couple–child dyad. This opens the scenario to a new dimension of health for the woman and the family based on an engaged fatherhood approach (Grau-Grau et al., 2022). Through participatory fatherhood and co-parenting policies, this approach leads to overcoming the cultural father–breadwinner/mother–caregiver model. Shared family caregiving, often made necessary in the pandemic era, brings the topic of fatherhood back to the attention of literature, health policy, and clinical practice. The topic of fatherhood in clinical practice, which has been explored by scholars since the 1970s (Fein, 1978; Kotelchuck et al., 1975; Lamb, 1979; Lamb & Lamb, 1976; Levy & Kotelchuck, 2022), has had a rather modest follow-up in terms of projects and further research. The only driver for the credibility of the paternal model in family care was the federal My Brother's Keeper program promoted by Barack Obama in 2014. This has pushed public health project lines toward projects and research that enhance parental functions even in the birth path (Dee & Penner, 2021; Harris, 2015). While services related to preconception, childbirth, and pueperium care still remain traditionally anchored in the exclusive domain of women, in clinical practice the paternal role is gaining increasing importance (Bowles et al., 2021). A paternal presence early in the birth journey generates benefits not only for the birth itself but also for life development and health as a whole (Condon et al., 2022; Kotelchuck, 2021).

The engaged fatherhood approach (see Andreasson et al., 2022; Caldwell et al., 2019; Gatrell et al., 2021), rediscovering a new centrality of the patient, creates space to intervene in the managerial and organizational ecosystems. A wider and more varied number of stakeholders than those traditionally contemplated come into play in the birth path network. In addition to the territorial facilities and birth points, there are national and supranational institutions, scientific societies, and professional orders that belong to varied categories (e.g., gynecologists, midwives, neonatologists, anesthesiologists, NICU nurses, associations that influence the pathway dynamics, Life Science companies, and ICT/service design experts).

The birth path, as a result, tends to be configured no longer as a sequential and linear delivery process that transforms inputs into outputs in a 'product-dominant logic' (Osborne, 2018; Osborne et al., 2021; Osborne et al., 2022) but, rather, as a Value Constellation in which each actor not only "adds value" but also reinvents it by redesigning roles and relationship systems (Freire & Sangiorgi, 2010; Michel et al., 2008; Normann, 2001; Vanhaverbeke & Cloodt, 2006). Thus, the value produced arises from a complex and multidimensional space in which different stakeholders interact with each other, societal values and norms, the local community, and service delivery processes (Skålén et al., 2015). The Value Constellation, therefore, is not required to recognize and activate co-production processes but, rather, is required to foster and govern them in their complex dynamics (Rubalcaba & Peralta, 2022; Strokosch & Osborne, 2020; Wirtz et al., 2021).

5.2 Distributed health literacy and empowerment in the birth path

The traditional value-generating sources in the birth path are represented by Health Literacy (HL) and empowerment. The WHO itself considers these two elements critical to improving women's health programs and inspiring legislative action at the international and national levels. Scientific studies have shown how HL influences health service behaviors and utilization, with consequences in terms of health outcomes and costs for the individual and the community (Nawabi et al., 2021; Palumbo et al., 2016). Individuals with inadequate health literacy (i.e., who use prevention less frequently and have greater difficulty self-managing their condition) have worse health outcomes (Magnani et al., 2018; Parekh et al., 2018; Stormacq et al., 2019).

In its broadest sense, HL has been generally considered as an international public health goal and understood as the degree to which individuals have the capacity to obtain, process, and understand basic health information and services needed to make appropriate health decisions

(Ratzan & Parker, 2000). In the context of the birth path, HL is understood as the set of cognitive and social skills that determine women's motivation and ability to access, understand, and use information in ways that promote and maintain their own and their children's health (Renkert & Nutbeam, 2001). Indeed, adequate health literacy increases the likelihood of identifying risk factors and, therefore, adopting healthier lifestyles (Jayasinghe et al., 2016; Kohan et al., 2008; Taggart et al., 2012).

Within the birth path as a Value Constellation, the importance of the social dimension of Health Literacy emerges (Sentell et al., 2017; Kendir & Breton, 2020; Stormacq et al., 2020) by providing not merely an understanding of the steps of the pathway, but a set of skills spread within the relational sphere of the couple. Thus, a distributed HL is configured, typically promoted, and tested in the field of chronicity (Finn & O'Fallon, 2017; Muscat et al, 2022a, 2022b), involving the family and the social community of reference. It also enables the empowerment of the couple by acting on the sharing of knowledge and understanding, access to and evaluation of information, as well as support for communication and decision-making.

In recent years, there has been a consolidated need for active participation and involvement of patients in healthcare decision-making processes in order to improve health outcomes, promote more informed access to healthcare services, and achieve benefits on healthcare spending, in terms of making facilities and services more efficient (Boivin et al., 2018; Brabers et al., 2017), although there are some difficulties related to cultural issues (Hawley & Morris, 2017). Patients, therefore, are conceived not as passive recipients but rather as active participants in care decision-making.

For the birth path, empowerment is a driving force for successful pregnancy and delivery (Crondahl & Eklund Karlsson, 2016). Its strategic profile is also emphasized, since the woman and couple are faced with completely new health-related decisions (Finbråten et al., 2020). In the proposed model, empowerment also takes a "distributed" view that includes a strong social dimension (Almunwar et al., 2015) in addition to personal and medical dimensions. Personal empowerment allows the woman and the couple to identify their needs; medical empowerment allows them to interact with the different players in the pathway who deliver the different health and social services; and social empowerment includes the sharing of information and experiences of women (Antoniak et al., 2019) and the related social community that can inspire pathways of improvement for the entire Value Constellation.

Expanding the boundaries of HL and empowerment generates a feeling of self-actualization and self-determination that allows the woman to interact, in a conscious manner, with the different actors in the relevant context and lavish the right psychological energy in a birth path with positive outcomes (Tavananezhad et al., 2022).

Finally, the distributed dimension of HL and empowerment makes it possible to address the complex health needs of the birth path while developing modern citizenship.

5.3 ICT as a clinical and managerial support tool

The effectiveness of Value Constellation for the birth path also depends heavily on the role of technologies in supporting the woman, the couple, and the entire organizational ecosystem (Nöjd et al., 2020). Technological solutions represent a powerful tool through which to establish contact and interaction with health professionals and health facilities, improve the quality and efficiency of care, increase health literacy, and carry out an educational and empowerment process (Agbo et al., 2019; Feldman et al., 2018; Latif et al., 2020; Patricio et al., 2020).

In the case of the birth path, greatly expanding the boundaries of women's and couples' empowerment is intervened by a variety of online applications that support improvement in terms of health management (Wu et al., 2020). Although most women seek information from clinical professionals, many use the Internet because they feel the information they receive from their doctor is unclear or to reinforce their current knowledge (Silva et al., 2019).

According to Mankuta et al. (2007), most of the information requested by women focuses on prenatal or intra-partum events, while other studies have found that the topic most frequently sought by women is that of complications during pregnancy. The use of a smartphone app represents, within the Value Constellation, a tool that facilitates HL and empowerment by generating good health outcomes in terms of appropriate patient behavior (Abdulrahman & Ganasegeran, 2019). In fact, many studies show how the use of these ICT aids is effective for smoking cessation, medication adherence, and blood pressure management (McLean, 2020; Whittaker et al., 2016; Shirzad et al., 2020; Shirzad et al., 2022; Tripp et al., 2014).

In addition, informational and decision-making empowerment allows the woman and couple to act on the cultural determinants of inappropriate use of cesarean section. This medical practice over the years has lost its emergent meaning by representing a type of choice that does not take into account real medical risk factors. In fact, over the years, improvements in surgical technologies have generated the belief that cesarean section is risk-free, whereas data from the medical literature suggest the procedure is associated with risks to women's health that increase in the case of multiple cesarean sections (Sandall et al., 2018).

Among the elements that can affect women's choice to resort to cesarean section is the psychological aspect that, if not managed properly, can result in pathological manifestations such as tocophobia (Winter, 2018; O'Connell et al., 2021). This refers to intense anxiety and dread of childbirth that, when it occurs during pregnancy, can cause the woman to avoid childbirth itself by opting for cesarean section (Kanellopoulos & Gourounti, 2022).

The unconscious choice of cesarean section generates "value destruction" both at the individual level, because an unnecessary surgical practice is used, and at the societal level, because it contributes to a health policy that does not preserve the health of the mother and child.

Technology and modern communication methods, through sustainable and easy-to-use co-production tools, can be helpful in supporting HL and couple empowerment.

The many apps offered by iOS and Android platforms, made available to women to provide support during pregnancy, are also useful on the organizational level through data collection, information exchange, and improved outcomes in terms of health service utilization and health outcomes (see Musgrave et al., 2020; Overdijkink et al., 2018).

Value Constellation, in fact, can be supported in its digital development by leveraging the benefits offered by cloud computing, Big Data, Artificial Intelligence (AI), and the Internet of Things (IoT).

An effective response to improving the birth path can come from Machine Learning, a branch of Artificial Intelligence that deals with creating systems that learn or improve performance based on the data used (de l'Espinay et al., 2019; Moreira et al., 2019). The use of such technology may be of particular interest because it would allow more accurate re-interpretation and interpretation of the amount of data that are produced at all stages of the birth pathway. In particular, the implementation of a Big Data Analytics ICT solution, based on Machine Learning algorithms, is capable of creating a predictive environment for risk assessment (Razzak et al., 2020). Data on clinical and extra-clinical variables that correlate with natural childbirth and cesarean section could be analyzed, captured, and processed by a digital platform that, through the use of predictive algorithms, is able to estimate each patient's mode of delivery. The platform would be a useful tool for the realization of birth pathway optimization and for clinical and managerial decision support.

5.4 Conclusions and implications for academic literature on healthcare organizations

The study has implications for the literature on healthcare organizations, as it paves the way for new strands of research potentially generating innovation in terms of health paradigm and organizational and management models underlying the birth path.

The multidisciplinary reading key delivers a sharp snapshot of the complexity of healthcare phenomena that increasingly require dialog between different scientific domains and between the multiple knowledges that are increasingly mutually indispensable in professional dominated healthcare organizations.

The first implication provided by the study is the rethinking of the health paradigm underlying the birth path. The pandemic crisis that has gripped humanity with the devastating and unexpected impact of a "black swan" (Teleb, 2007) has deconstructed many of the elements of health policy and organization that had been established over the years (Wind et al., 2020). As a result, the bio-psycho-social health paradigm has been enriched with an additional and broader dimension that leads to the declination of health as an essential asset for a country's security. In a vision of total health, the figure of the couple and the fatherhood approach become central to the birth path, which succeed in recapturing the physiological and conscious dimension of birth while supporting, at the same time, the change in gender roles involved in care.

The renewed paradigm of health brings with it the second implication of the research, which concerns the organizational and managerial implications of this for the Health System. In particular, the research highlights how, in the birth path, value is not generated in a linear manner through an ordered sequence of actions. Rather, it derives from a complex and broader system of relationships that, in a redesigned Value Constellation, involves new stakeholders not traditionally contemplated. The challenge facing management and organizational scholars is to co-design, in a distinctly multidisciplinary terrain, the structural, relational, and technological determinants that can give the Value Constellation of the birth path the value-generating energy for the couple, the care team, and society as a whole.

Finally, the third implication concerns exploration and research insights useful to the disciplinary domain of information systems called upon to support social and managerial change. Indeed, they are entrusted with the task of studying technological solutions that can strengthen the Value Constellation's autopoietic capacity by systemizing cultural, clinical, and organizational aspects.

References

Abdulrahman, S. A., & Ganasegeran, K. (2019). m-Health in public health practice: a constellation of current evidence. In *Telemedicine technologies* (pp. 171–182). Academic Press.

Agbo, C. C., Mahmoud, Q. H., & Eklund, J. M. (2019). Blockchain technology in healthcare: a systematic review. In *Healthcare* (Vol. 7, No. 2, p. 56). MDPI.

Alford, J. (2016). Co-production, interdependence and publicness: extending public service-dominant logic. *Public Management Review*, 18(5), 673–691.

Almunawar, M. N., Anshari, M., & Younis, M. Z. (2015). Incorporating customer empowerment in mobile health. *Health Policy and Technology*, 4(4), 312–319.

Andreasson, J., Tarrant, A., Johansson, T., & Ladlow, L. (2022). Perceptions of gender equality and engaged fatherhood among young fathers: parenthood and the welfare state in Sweden and the UK. *Families, Relationships and Societies*, 1–18.

Antoniak, M., Mimno, D., & Levy, K. (2019). Narrative paths and negotiation of power in birth stories. *Proceedings of the ACM on Human-Computer Interaction*, 3(CSCW), 1–27.

Boivin, A., L'Espérance, A., Gauvin, F. P., Dumez, V., Macaulay, A. C., Lehoux, P., & Abelson, J. (2018). Patient and public engagement in research and health system decision making: a systematic review of evaluation tools. *Health Expectations*, *21*(6), 1075–1084.

Bowles, H. R., Kotelchuck, M., & Grau-Grau, M. (2021). Reducing barriers to engaged fatherhood: three principles for promoting gender equity in parenting. *Engaged fatherhood for men, families and gender equality* (pp. 299–325). Springer, Cham.

Brabers, A. E., Rademakers, J. J., Groenewegen, P. P., Van Dijk, L., & De Jong, J. D. (2017). What role does health literacy play in patients' involvement in medical decision-making?. *PloS One*, *12*(3), e0173316.

Caldwell, C. H., Tsuchiya, K., Assari, S., & Thomas, A. (2019). Fatherhood as a social context for reducing men's health disparities: lessons learned from the fathers and sons program. In Griffith, D.M., Bruce, M.A., &Thorpe, R.J. (Eds.), *Men's health equity: A handbook* (pp. 42–56). Routledge/Taylor & Francis Group. 10.4324/9781315167428-4

Cannito, M. (2020). Beyond "traditional" and "new": An attempt of redefinition of contemporary fatherhoods through discursive practices and practices of care. *Men and Masculinities*, *23*(3–4), 661–679.

Condon, E. M., Dettmer, A., Baker, E., McFaul, C., & Stover, C. S. (2022). Early life adversity and males: biology, behavior, and implications for fathers' parenting. *Neuroscience & Biobehavioral Reviews*, *135*, 104531. 10.1016/j.neubiorev.2022.104531

Crondahl, K., & Eklund Karlsson, L. (2016). The nexus between health literacy and empowerment: a scoping review. *Sage Open*, *6*(2), 2158244016646410.

Cui, T., & Osborne, S. P. (2022). Unpacking value destruction at the intersection between public and private value. *Public Administration*, 1–20. 10.1111/padm.12850

de l'Espinay, A., Sauvage, C., Buronfosse, A., Billuart, O., Lajonchère, J. P., & Azria, E. (2019). Machine learning to anticipate delivery room activity?. *Journal of Gynecology Obstetrics and Human Reproduction*, *48*(3), 141–142.

Dee, T. S., & Penner, E. K. (2021). My brother's keeper? The impact of targeted educational supports. *Journal of Policy Analysis and Management*, *40*(4), 1171–1196.

Fein, R. A. (1978). Research on fathering: social policy and an emergent perspective. *Journal of Social Issues*, *34*(1), 122–135.

Feldman, S. S., Buchalter, S., & Hayes, L. W. (2018). Health information technology in healthcare quality and patient safety: literature review. *JMIR Medical Informatics*, *6*(2), e10264.

Finbråten, H. S., Guttersrud, Ø., Nordström, G., Pettersen, K. S., Trollvik, A., & Wilde-Larsson, B. (2020). Explaining variance in health literacy among people with type 2 diabetes: the association between health literacy and health behaviour and empowerment. *BMC Public Health*, *20*(1), 1–12.

Finn, S., & O'Fallon, L. (2017). The emergence of environmental health literacy—from its roots to its future potential. *Environmental Health Perspectives*, *125*(4), 495–501.

Freire, K., & Sangiorgi, D. (2010). Service design and healthcare innovation: From consumption to co-production to co-creation. In *Service Design and Service Innovation conference* (pp. 39–50). Linköping Electronic Conference Proceedings.

Gatrell, C., Ladge, J. J., & Powell, G. N. (2022). A review of fatherhood and employment: introducing new perspectives for management research. *Journal of Management Studies*, *59*. 10.1111/joms.12771

Grau-Grau, M., las Heras Maestro, M., & Riley Bowles, H. (2022). Engaged fatherhood for men, families and gender equality: healthcare, social policy, and work perspectives, Springer.

Harris, F. C. (2015). The challenges of my brother's keeper. *Governance Studies at Brookings*. Washington, DC: The Brookings Institution. Retrieved from https://www.brookings. edu/wp-content/uploads/2016/07/my_brothers_keeper.pdf.

Hawley, S. T., & Morris, A. M. (2017). Cultural challenges to engaging patients in shared decision making. *Patient education and counseling, 100*(1), 18–24.

Jayasinghe, U. W., Harris, M. F., Parker, S. M., Litt, J., van Driel, M., Mazza, D., ... & Taylor, R. (2016). The impact of health literacy and life style risk factors on health-related quality of life of Australian patients. *Health and Quality of Life Outcomes, 14*(1), 1–13.

Kanellopoulos, D., & Gourounti, K. (2022). Tocophobia and women's desire for a caesarean section: a systematic review. *Maedica A Journal of Clinical Medicine, 17*(1), 186–193. 10.26574/maedica.2022.17.1.186

Keeling, D. I., Keeling, K., de Ruyter, K., & Laing, A. (2021). How value co-creation and co-destruction unfolds: a longitudinal perspective on dialogic engagement in health services interactions. *Journal of the Academy of Marketing Science, 49*(2), 236–257.

Kendir, C., & Breton, E. (2020). Health literacy: from a property of individuals to one of communities. *International Journal of Environmental Research and public health, 17*(5), 1601.

Kohan, S., Ghasemi, S., & Dodangeh, M. (2008). Associations between maternal health literacy and prenatal care and pregnancy outcome. *Iranian Journal of Nursing and Midwifery Research, 12*(4).

Kotelchuck, M. (2021). The impact of father's health on reproductive and infant health and development. *Engaged Fatherhood for Men, Families and Gender Equality* (pp. 31–61). Cham: Springer.

Kotelchuck, M., Zelazo, P. R., Kagan, J., & Spelke, E. (1975). Infant reaction to parental separations when left with familiar and unfamiliar adults. *The Journal of Genetic Psychology, 126*(2), 255–262.

Lamb, M. E. (1979). Paternal influences and the father's role: a personal perspective. *American Psychologist, 34*(10), 938.

Lamb, M. E., & Lamb, J. E. (1976). The nature and importance of the father-infant relationship. *Family Coordinator, 25*(4), 379–385. 10.2307/582850

Latif, S., Qadir, J., Qayyum, A., Usama, M., & Younis, S. (2020). Speech technology for healthcare: opportunities, challenges, and state of the art. *IEEE Reviews in Biomedical Engineering, 14*, 342–356.

Levy, R. A., & Kotelchuck, M. (2022). Fatherhood and reproductive health in the antenatal period: from men's voices to clinical practice. In *Engaged Fatherhood for Men, Families and Gender Equality* (pp. 111–137). Cham: Springer.

Magnani, J. W., Mujahid, M. S., Aronow, H. D., Cené, C. W., Dickson, V. V., Havranek, E., ... & Willey, J. Z. (2018). Health literacy and cardiovascular disease: fundamental relevance to primary and secondary prevention: a scientific statement from the American Heart Association. *Circulation, 138*(2), e48–e74.

Mankuta, D., Vinker, S., Shapira, S., Laufer, N., & Shveiky, D. (2007). The use of a perinatal internet consultation forum in Israel. *BJOG: An International Journal of Obstetrics & Gynaecology, 114*(1), 108–110.

McLean, A. (2020). mHealth Apps as Effective Persuasive Health Technology: Contextualizing the "Necessary" Functionalities. *JMIR nursing, 3*(1), e19302.

Michel, S., Vargo, S. L., & Lusch, R. F. (2008). Reconfiguration of the conceptual landscape: a tribute to the service logic of Richard Normann. *Journal of the Academy of Marketing Science, 36*(1), 152–155.

Moreira, M. W., Rodrigues, J. J., Furtado, V., Mavromoustakis, C. X., Kumar, N., & Wougang, I. (2019). Fetal birth weight estimation in high-risk pregnancies through machine learning techniques. In *ICC 2019–2019 IEEE International Conference on Communications (ICC)* (pp. 1–6). IEEE.

Muscat, D. M., Cvejic, E., Bell, K., Smith, J., Morris, G. M., Jansen, J., ... & McCaffery, K. (2022a). The impact of health literacy on psychosocial and behavioural outcomes among people at low risk of cardiovascular disease. *Preventive Medicine, 156,* 106980.

Muscat, D. M., Gessler, D., Ayre, J., Norgaard, O., Heuck, I. R., Haar, S., & Maindal, H. T. (2022b). Seeking a deeper understanding of 'distributed health literacy': a systematic review. *Health Expectations, 25*(3), 856–868.

Musgrave, L. M., Kizirian, N. V., Homer, C. S., & Gordon, A. (2020). Mobile phone apps in Australia for improving pregnancy outcomes: systematic search on app stores. *JMIR mHealth and uHealth, 8*(11), e22340.

Nawabi, F., Krebs, F., Vennedey, V., Shukri, A., Lorenz, L., & Stock, S. (2021). Health literacy in pregnant women: a systematic review. *International Journal of Environmental Research and Public Health, 18*(7), 3847.

Nöjd, S., Trischler, J. W., Otterbring, T., Andersson, P. K., & Wästlund, E. (2020). Bridging the valuescape with digital technology: a mixed methods study on customers' value creation process in the physical retail space. *Journal of Retailing and Consumer Services, 56,* 102161.

Normann, R. (2001). *Reframing business: when the map changes the landscape.* John Wiley & Sons.

O'Connell, M. A., Khashan, A. S., Leahy-Warren, P., Stewart, F., & O'Neill, S. M. (2021). Interventions for fear of childbirth including tocophobia. *Cochrane Database of Systematic Reviews, 7*(7), CD013321. 10.1002/14651858.CD013321.pub2

OASI report (2021). *Osservatorio sulle Aziende e sul Sistema sanitario Italiano* [Observatory on Companies and the Italian Health System]. CERGAS Bocconi.

Osborne, S. P. (2018). From public service-dominant logic to public service logic: are public service organizations capable of co-production and value co-creation?. *Public Management Review, 20*(2), 225–231.

Osborne, S. P., Nasi, G., & Powell, M. (2021). Beyond co-production: value creation and public services. *Public Administration, 99*(4), 641–657.

Osborne, S., Powell, M. G. H., Cui, T., & Strokosch, K. (2022). Value creation in the public service ecosystem: an integrative framework. *Public Administration Review, 82*(4), 634–645. 10.1111/puar.13474

Overdijkink, S. B., Velu, A. V., Rosman, A. N., Van Beukering, M. D., Kok, M., & Steegers-Theunissen, R. P. (2018). The usability and effectiveness of mobile health technology–based lifestyle and medical intervention apps supporting health care during pregnancy: systematic review. *JMIR mHealth and uHealth, 6*(4), e8834.

Palumbo, R., Annarumma, C., Adinolfi, P., Musella, M., & Piscopo, G. (2016). The Italian Health Literacy Project: insights from the assessment of health literacy skills in Italy. *Health Policy, 120*(9), 1087–1094.

Parekh, N., Ali, K., Davies, K., & Rajkumar, C. (2018). Can supporting health literacy reduce medication-related harm in older adults?. *Therapeutic Advances in Drug Safety, 9*(3), 167–170.

Patricio, L., Sangiorgi, D., Mahr, D., Čaić, M., Kalantari, S., & Sundar, S. (2020). Leveraging service design for healthcare transformation: toward people-centered, integrated, and technology-enabled healthcare systems. *Journal of Service Management, 31*(5), 889–909.

Ratzan, S. C., & Parker, R. M. (2000). Health literacy. *National library of medicine current bibliographies in medicine*. Bethesda: National Institutes of Health, US Department of Health and Human Services.

Razzak, M. I., Imran, M., & Xu, G. (2020). Big data analytics for preventive medicine. *Neural Computing and Applications*, *32*(9), 4417–4451.

Renkert, S., & Nutbeam, D. (2001). Opportunities to improve maternal health literacy through antenatal education: an exploratory study. *Health Promotion International*, *16*(4), 381–388.

Rubalcaba, L., & Peralta, A. (2022). Value processes and lifecycles in networks for public service innovation. *Public Management Review*, 1–20.

Sandall, J., Tribe, R. M., Avery, L., Mola, G., Visser, G. H., Homer, C. S., ... & Temmerman, M. (2018). Short-term and long-term effects of caesarean section on the health of women and children. *The Lancet*, *392*(10155), 1349–1357.

Sentell, T., Pitt, R., & Buchthal, O. V. (2017). Health literacy in a social context: review of quantitative evidence. *HLRP: Health Literacy Research and Practice*, *1*(2), e41–e70.

Shirzad, A., Khalesi, Z. B., & Niknami, M. (2022). The effect of a mobile-based education app on fear of childbirth in pregnant women. *International Journal of Childbirth*.

Shirzad, M., Shakibazadeh, E., Rahimi Foroushani, A., Abedini, M., Poursharifi, H., & Babaei, S. (2020). Effect of "motivational interviewing" and "information, motivation, and behavioral skills" counseling interventions on choosing the mode of delivery in pregnant women: a study protocol for a randomized controlled trial. *Trials*, *21*(1), 1–10.

Silva, R. M. D., Brasil, C. C. P., Bezerra, I. C., & Queiroz, F. F. D. S. N. (2019). Mobile health technology for gestational care: evaluation of the GestAção's App. *Revista Brasileira de Enfermagem*, *72*, 266–273.

Skålén, P., Gummerus, J., Von Koskull, C., & Magnusson, P. R. (2015). Exploring value propositions and service innovation: a service-dominant logic study. *Journal of the Academy of Marketing Science*, *43*(2), 137–158.

Stormacq, C., Van den Broucke, S., & Wosinski, J. (2019). Does health literacy mediate the relationship between socioeconomic status and health disparities? Integrative review. *Health Promotion International*, *34*(5), e1–e17.

Stormacq, C., Wosinski, J., Boillat, E., & Van den Broucke, S. (2020). Effects of health literacy interventions on health-related outcomes in socioeconomically disadvantaged adults living in the community: a systematic review. *JBI Evidence Synthesis*, *18*(7), 1389–1469.

Strokosch, K., & Osborne, S. P. (2020). Co-experience, co-production and co-governance: an ecosystem approach to the analysis of value creation. *Policy & Politics*, *48*(3), 425–442.

Taggart, J., Williams, A., Dennis, S., Newall, A., Shortus, T., Zwar, N., ... & Harris, M. F. (2012). A systematic review of interventions in primary care to improve health literacy for chronic disease behavioral risk factors. *BMC Family Practice*, *13*(1), 1–12.

Taleb, N. N. (2007). Black swans and the domains of statistics. *The American Statistician*, *61*(3), 198–200.

Tavananezhad, N., Bolbanabad, A. M., Ghelichkhani, F., Effati-Daryani, F., & Mirghafourvand, M. (2022). The relationship between health literacy and empowerment in pregnant women: a cross-sectional study. *BMC Pregnancy and Childbirth*, *22*(1), 1–9.

Tripp, N., Hainey, K., Liu, A., Poulton, A., Peek, M., Kim, J., & Nanan, R. (2014). An emerging model of maternity care: smartphone, midwife, doctor?. *Women and Birth*, *27*(1), 64–67.

Vanhaverbeke, W., & Cloodt, M. (2006). Open innovation in value networks. *Open Innovation: Researching a New Paradigm* (pp. 258–281). Oxford University Press.

Wexler, A., Davoudi, A., Weissenbacher, D., Choi, R., O'Connor, K., Cummings, H., & Gonzalez-Hernandez, G. (2020). Pregnancy and health in the age of the internet: a content analysis of online "birth club" forums. *PloS One*, *15*(4), e0230947.

Whittaker, R., McRobbie, H., Bullen, C., Rodgers, A., & Gu, Y. (2016). Mobile phone-based interventions for smoking cessation. *Cochrane Database of Systematic Reviews*, *4*(4), CD006611. 10.1002/14651858.CD006611.pub4

Wind, T. R., Rijkeboer, M., Andersson, G., & Riper, H. (2020). The COVID-19 pandemic: the 'black swan'for mental health care and a turning point for e-health. *Internet Interventions*, *20*, 100317. 10.1016/j.invent.2020.100317

Winter, G. F. (2018). Tocophobia. *British Journal of Midwifery*, *26*(2), 129–129.

Wirtz, B. W., Kubin, P. R., & Weyerer, J. C. (2021). Business model innovation in the public sector: an integrative framework. *Public Management Review*, 1–36.

Wu, H., Sun, W., Huang, X., Yu, S., Wang, H., Bi, X., ... & Ming, W. K. (2020). Online antenatal care during the COVID-19 pandemic: opportunities and challenges. *Journal of Medical Internet Research*, *22*(7), e19916.

Index

Note: **Bold** page numbers refer to tables and *italic* page numbers refer to figures.

Adinolfi, P. 20
administrative healthcare cycle 19
Almunawar, M. N. 7
autonomous professional organizations 22

baby-bust 7
birthing care models 10–11
birth path 1; access to 43–44, *45*; aspects and characteristics of 4–5; cesarean section 5, 51–59; effective and efficient 7; health literacy and empowerment in 90–92; labor and delivery phase 47–49, *48*; low-risk pregnancy 44–47, *46*; medicalization of pregnancy 51–59; medium-/high-risk pregnancy 44–47, *46*; organizational models 5; postpartum hemorrhage 49; preconception phase 41–43, *43*; puerperium phase 49–51, *50*; redesigning 32–34, 87–90; social determinants and epidemiology of 5–7; stages of 41; technologies and digital tools 7–10; Value Constellation for 87, *88*, 92–94; value systems in *42*
BPI *see* Business Process Improvement
BPR *see* Business Process Reengineering
brain-intensive organizations 22
Business Process Improvement 32
Business Process Reengineering 32–33, 87

care process 30–31
case studies 69–70; Certificates of Birth Assistance 73–75; cesareans 78–79; data analysis 75–81; data collection 73–75; Hospital Discharge Cards 73–75; Italian context 70–71; logistic regression 79; maternal age 77; mode of delivery/labor 76; previous conceptions 78; professional condition 77; results of 81–82; T.R.E.E. model 71–73
CeDAPs *see* Certificates of Birth Assistance
Certificates of Birth Assistance 73–75
cesarean section 5, 6; cultural factors 57; economic factors 56–57; elective/programmed 49; increase in 69; infant factors 54; maternal decision-making 55–56; maternal factors 54; and medicalization of pregnancy 51–59; medical risk factors 54; obstetric factors 54; organizational factors 54; physician's assessment 55; Robson's Classification system 53, **53**; social and demographic factors 54–55; surgical technologies 8
CG *see* Clinical Governance
Champy, J. 32
childbirth 1, 10–11; cesarean section **76–79**, 82; masters of 4; medicalization of 4; mode of 69; natural 1, 56, **76–79**, 81, 82; obstetrical characteristics 53; pain in 4; as physiological event 89 *see also* birthing care models; birth path
clinical culture 22
Clinical Governance 29
cloning-type control 25
cultural factors, cesarean section 57
custodial healthcare cycle 19

Davenport, T. H. 32
death/mortality rates 10, 34

decision-making: pregnant women 7–8, 92; professionals 22, 23
Degani, N. 54
delivery: choice of mode 7, 76; health care 52; labor and 47–49, *48*
Diagnosis Related Group 57
digital technologies 7–10, 92–93
Disease Management 29
Donaldson, L. J. 29
DRG *see* Diagnosis Related Group

economic factors, cesarean section 56–57
elective/programmed cesarean section 49
employment status and health outcomes 6
empowerment 7, 90–92
European women 6
Evidence-Based Medicine 29

fetal expulsion 48–49
financial incentives, cesarean section 56–57
Freidson, E. 22

gynecologist 41, 42, 71, 83

Hammer, M. 32
healthcare: care process 30–31; Clinical Governance 29; complexity 18–19; delivery system 52; Disease Management 29; functional cycles 19; managerial 18–21; myths 20–21; organizational 18, 21–25, 93–94; pandemic crisis 94; processes 25–28; Process Management 29–30; redesigning and birth path challenges 32–34; reforms 19–21; variability in 18–19
health literacy and empowerment 90–92
health policy 5
hemorrhage 10, 49
heteronomous professional organizations 22
high-tech birthing model 10–11
Hospital Discharge Cards 73–75

ICT *see* Information and Communication Technology
IGME *see* Inter-Agency Group for Child Mortality Estimation
industrialized countries, pregnancy in 9
inequalities 5
infant factors, cesarean section 54
informational pregnancy apps 9

Information and Communication Technology 32–34; birth path 93; cesarean section, choice of 92–93; decision-making empowerment 92; surgical technologies 8, 92; Value Constellation 87, *88*, 92–94
instrumental pregnancy apps 9
interactive pregnancy apps 9
Inter-Agency Group for Child Mortality Estimation 10
intermediate birthing model 11
Internet-based (eHealth) information 8
Interprofessional Collaboration 31
IPC *see* Interprofessional Collaboration
Istituto Superiore di Sanità 71
Italian context 70–71
Italian hospitals 69
Italy, childbirths 6–7

Khan, U. 33
Kramer, M. S. 5–6
Kraschnewski, J. L. 8

labor and delivery phase 47–49, *48*
Lega, F. 33
Le, K. 5
low-risk pregnancy pathway 44–47

managerial culture 23
managerial healthcare 18; complexity and variability of 18–19; reforms and myths 19–21
Mankuta, D. 92
masters of childbirth 4
maternal decision-making, cesarean section 55–56
maternal education 5–6, 71; mobile app 8–9
maternal factors, cesarean section 54
maternal mortality 10, 11
medical healthcare cycle 19
medicalization of pregnancy 51–59
medicalized birthing model 11
medical perspective, empowerment 7
medium-/high-risk pregnancy pathway 44–47
Midwifery2030 Pathway 34
midwifery model 34
migrant women 6
Mintzberg, H. 23
mobile apps 8–9
monocentrism myth 20
mortality rates 10, 34

multidisciplinarity action 31
multidisciplinary debate 10–11
myths 20–21

natural childbirth 1, 56, **76–79**, 81, 82
neonatal complications 54
neonatal mortality 10–11
New Public Governance 21, 25, 87
New Public Management 19–20
Nguyen, M. 5

obesity 6
obstetrical risk 47–48
obstetric factors 54
online applications 7
operational core 24
operative vaginal delivery 6
organizational factors, cesarean section 56
organizational healthcare 21–25; challenges 25; clinical activities 18–19; operational core 24; patient-centeredness approach 29–32; processes 72–73; supporting staffs 24; technostructure 24; top management 24; variability 18
organizational individualism myth 20–21
organizational models, birth path 5
Overgaard, C. 6

pain in childbirth 4
patient-centeredness healthcare 29–32
personal beliefs, cesarean section 57
personal perspective, empowerment 7
physician's assessment, cesarean section 55
pigeonholing 23
Porter, M. E. 26
postpartum hemorrhage 49
preconception phase 41–43, *42*, *43*
pregnancy 1; access to birth path 43–44, *45*; apps 8–9; employment status and health outcomes 6; formative moment 7; high-risk 11; inequalities in 5; labor and delivery phase 47–49, *48*; low-risk pathway 44–47; maternal education 5–6, 71; medium-/high-risk pathway 44–47 *see also* birth path
prenatal services 5
primary clinical-care processes 26–27, *28*
Process Management 29–30
professionals/profession/professionalism 19, 22; bureaucracy *23*, 24–25; clinical culture 22; interprofessional collaboration 31; managerial culture 23; multidisciplinarity action 31; trans-disciplinarity action 31
puerperium phase 49–51, *50*
pure radical approach 33

radical-contingent approach 33
rationalistic myth 20
redesigning birthpath 32–34, 87; fatherhood approach 89–90; health literacy and empowerment in 90–92; ICT tools 90–92; management of COVID-19 87; primary stimulus for 89; product dominant logic 90; Value Constellation for 87, *88*, 92–94
redesigning structure organization 4
reengineering process 32–33
reforms, healthcare 19–21
Robson's Classification system 53, **53**

Scally, G. 29
Scott, W. R. 22
SDOs *see* Hospital Discharge Cards
Sikich, N. 54
smartphone app 8–9, 92
smartphone (mHealth) information 8
social and demographic factors, cesarean section 54–55
social determinants and epidemiology 5–7
social networking apps 9
social perspective, empowerment 7
socioeconomic disadvantages 6
socio-medical integration 25
supporting health processes 26–27, *28*
supporting staffs 24
supportive administrative processes 26–27, *28*
surgical technologies 8, 92

technicism myth 20
technologies and digital tools 7–10; informational pregnancy apps 9; instrumental pregnancy apps 9; interactive pregnancy apps 9; online applications 7; smartphone app 8–9; social networking apps 9; surgical technologies 8; tracking women's behaviors 9 *see also* Information and Communication Technology
technostructure 24
top management 24
trans-disciplinarity action 31

T.R.E.E. (Targeted exploration, Reconfiguration, Evaluation, and Exhibition) model 71–73

UK Health Plan 29
United Nations agencies 10
universalism myth 20

Value Constellation 87, *88*, 92–94

Wagner, M. 10–11
WHO *see* World Health Organization
Wilensky, H. L. 22
World Health Organization 10, 31; cesarean section 52

Printed in the United States
by Baker & Taylor Publisher Services